S0-BOC-216

Zambia and the Decline of Kaunda 1984-1998

Front cover photograph of Stanley Chiwambo, Zambian UN peacekeeping soldier.
Peacekeeping remains one of Kaunda's enduring legacies.

ZAMBIA AND THE DECLINE OF KAUNDA 1984-1998

Stephen Chan

Edited by
Craig Clancy

African Studies
Volume 57

The Edwin Mellen Press
Lewiston•Queenston•Lampeter

Library of Congress Cataloging-in-Publication Data

Chan, Stephen.
Zambia and the Decline of Kaunda 1984-1998.
Edited by Craig Clancy.

ISBN 0-7734-7504-4 (hard)

This is volume 57 in the continuing series
African Studies
Volume 57 ISBN 0-7734-7504-4
AS Series ISBN 0-88946-175-9

A CIP catalog record for this book is available from the British Library.

The Edwin Mellen Press
Box 450
Lewiston, New York
USA 14092-0450

The Edwin Mellen Press
Box 67
Queenston, Ontario
CANADA L0S 1L0

The Edwin Mellen Press, Ltd.
Lampeter, Ceredigion, Wales
UNITED KINGDOM SA48 8LT

Printed in the United States of America

TO MY PARENTS
SYLVIA AND KENNETH

TABLE OF CONTENTS

PART II

FOREWORD

I have both hosted and supported Stephen Chan's research in Zambia. His visits, unexpected, always original in their research methods and results, were a pleasure to all his friends in this country. He has become the most prolific and authoritative interpreter of Kenneth Kaunda and of Zambian politics at large. This collection of essays forms a stage-by-stage intellectual record – a history – of the process whereby this was achieved. Stephen Chan lived in Zambia from 1980 to 1985, and has returned annually since then. I know he has silently observed the downward fortune of his beloved University of Zambia with some sorrow. Maybe he will be asked to help it again one day. I should say, however, that ever since he arrived in Zambia, he has given back to the youth of the nation more than his research might ever have earned him. Even now, on weekends and in the evenings of every visit, he is busy teaching karate to the Zambian black belts, freely and, above all, reliably. That he will simply arrive every year is simply known. Scholars here and internationally may dispute his interpretations, but none of these has become a minor institution in this country, trekking, usually on foot, from appointment to appointment; holding court beside the colony of weaver birds at the Ridgeway Hotel; and, when finally left alone, his black hair over his shoulders, always in a dark suit, writing by the same birds. Any hidden microphone would be drowned out by their constant chatter. I smile at this. I see him brushing his hair back from his eyes in silent thought. I daresay most of these essays were first penned in those exact surroundings. It is probably fair to say, though Chan might dispute this, that some of his own current concerns and essays on international moral philosophy have their line of descent in his observations and astonishment at what Kaunda called a moral philosophy. If that is the case, then Zambia has provided the world with more than the Humanism of Kaunda. I know that the irony, at least, of such a thought would appeal to Stephen Chan. Those wicked grins have illuminated more than one Lusaka night.

Dr L. J. Chingambo
Lusaka
1999

PREFACE

The book's collection of essays serves two purposes. It is at once the working essays for Stephen Chan's authoritative *Zambia and Southern Africa: Image and Reality in Foreign Policy* (I.B.Tauris 1992); and it is a genealogy of an international origin of Kaunda, both as he was well regarded, and when he was deemed a grand anachronism. There were detractors of Kaunda from the start, Timothy Shaw of Canada in their vanguard; but Chan's accounts seem the most judicious, and unideological. He was the first of the non-Marxist scholars to provide a rounded critique of the man and, I daresay, the first to be surprised, if not finally pleased, at Kaunda's unexpected longevity as a gadfly to President Chiluba's lacklustre role of successor.

The first half of this collection appeared as an occasional paper of the University of Kent (Canterbury 1992), and thanks are due to Dr Keith Webb of Kent for his provision of the original discs. The essays here republished first appeared in the following journals and their editors are thanked:
Commonwealth, The Round Table, The New Zealand International Review, Wasafiri, (Osei-Hwedie & Ndulo eds.) *Issues in Zambian Development, Africa Institute Bulletin, Southern African yearbook of International Affairs 1996,* and as a 1991 Occasional Paper of the South African Institute of International Affairs.

Craig Clancy
Nottingham 1999

ACKNOWLEDGEMENTS

Janet Elkington prepared the new collection for formatting and publication; and The Nottingham Trent University both provided me with the wherewithal to assist this project as well as financing Chan's travel to Zambia for the last two essays in this collection. Earlier research by Chan in Zambia was financed by the ESRC, the US Institute of Peace, the Nuffield Foundation, and the University of Kent. He would like me, I am sure, to thank them all on his behalf.

PART 1

THE DECLINE OF KAUNDA : ESSAYS OF PRAISE AND COMPLAINT 1983-1989

Introduction

I first took a deep interest in Kenneth Kaunda in 1979, during the Commonwealth Heads of Government Meeting in Lusaka and the subsequent Lancaster House negotiations on the independence of Zimbabwe. At that time, I was working for the Commonwealth Secretariat and observed the skillful way in which Kaunda was slotted into the stratagems of the Commonwealth Secretary-General, Shridath Ramphal. It did not occur to me that, outside this Commonwealth context, Kaunda might not live up to the received image I and many of my colleagues and friends in all parts of the world had of him. That received image, of a noble man of peace and negotiation, was strong and lingers even today. His philosophy of `humanism' seemed, without any investigation, reasonable ammunition to use as a riposte against those who considered African social thought to be chauvinistic, crude, and not up to the modernising needs of the twentieth century. To use a modern term, Kaunda had developed 'good PR'.

This image of Kaunda lingered even after I went to live in Zambia in 1980. The country had just emerged from confrontation with Rhodesia and it seemed Kaunda should be given a chance to restore Zambia's fortunes. Not that, on the surface, those fortunes seemed eroded. In Lusaka at least, the standard of living was higher than in most African countries I had visited. There was even a higher class of shanty or squatter compound. I wrote on the 1983 Zambian elections, when

Kaunda was convincingly returned, and it seemed he had the confidence of the Zambian people in his efforts.

A look at the figures behind the confidence and calm suggested, however, very grave difficulties ahead. Even then, it was possible to blame market trends over which Kaunda and his government had no control. Moreover, in foreign policy, the field I was chiefly interested in, his record looked good and, if nothing else, the last thing that seemed doubtful was the man's sincerity. This feeling persisted in 1984 after having, at Adrian Wood's behest (Dr. Wood is now at Huddersfield Polytechnic, but was then a colleague at the University of Zambia), written a brief study of Kaunda's foreign policy. I defended (and still do) Kaunda from critiques of his career by scholars such as Canada's Timothy Shaw. But, from that exercise, I learnt how deeply - even if, as I felt, wrongly - Kaunda could be criticised and faulted.

I sent my article on Kaunda's foreign policy to William Tordoff at Manchester University, suggesting I might edit a book on opposing views of Kaunda; but Tordoff replied that the time was ripe for a full-length study of Kaunda's foreign policy. I began this project, but took until 1991 to complete it (*Kaunda and Southern Africa: Image and Reality in Foreign Policy,* London: I.B. Tauris, 1991). Along the way, I wrote several exploratory essays. Some of these are what have been collected together in this short monograph. The more I research, thought and wrote, however, the more it seemed apparent that Kaunda's received image simply could not be sustained. The longer I lived in Zambia or kept close contacts with it after I left, the more I traced the genealogy of its decline, and the more I was able to perceive the same forms of decision-making in foreign policy as in an increasingly disastrous domestic policy. These collected essays, which I used as personal working papers for the final book, reflect in the first instance the received and great image of Kaunda; they then start to defend him against criticism; they then start finding weaknesses and faults of their own; and they end as commentaries on his style and judgement which are highly critical. The last two essays attempt this in literary form first of all, and then as an investigation of a failed coup attempt. More

Substantial academic work on these last themes is found in the book.

Also in the book is a very detailed exposition of my arguments against the structuralist school of thought, led by Timothy Shaw. I now think Kaunda is highly vulnerable to sustained criticism, but the first major attempt to accomplish this was flawed. The method and results of my own criticism are, again, available from the book.

As working papers, these essays have the value of signposts in an intellectual odyssey and are therefore, for those interested in how thought passes through various stages, a companion to the book. They are offered only in that light and not as accomplished or complete pieces in their own right. Nevertheless, certain acknowledgements are due to those who were necessary to see even this modest project to the light of day. Thanks are due to the editors of *Commonwealth, The Round Table, New Zealand International Review, Wasafiri, Issues in Zambian Development* (eds. Osei-Hwedie and Ndulo, Roxbury, Mass: Omenana, 1985) and the organisers of the 1989 BISA/ISA Joint Convention, where these essays first appeared or were read. Versions of some essays have appeared in my books, *Issues in International Relations: A View From Africa,* and *Exporting Apartheid: Foreign Policies in Southern Africa 1978-1988*, both published by Macmillan (1987 and 1990).

X FOR THE EAGLE (1983)

In the week that US forces invaded Grenada, Kenneth Kaunda was re-elected President of Zambia with 93 per cent of the popular vote-an improvement over the 81 per cent he scored in 1978.

Speaking to foreign correspondents before the announcement of the final results, Kaunda commented that the editorial in the *Times of Zambia*, which described President Reagan as a rogue for invading Grenada, was in bad taste. He, himself, would not wish to be called a rogue by people who disagreed with his policies. The US President, by the same token, should not be attacked as an individual - although his policies should be.

This was Kaunda at his most infuriatingly reasonable. Ever since Zambia's independence, 19 years ago, he has been widely admired as a sincere and compassionate man, convinced of the Christian vision of righteousness and justice.

At the same time, observers have detected ruthlessness and steel beneath the public image; and have pointed also to the small circle of men who monopolise the powerful posts of the land, and who depend on the President as the linchpin of their tenure.

Certainly, in his latest book, *Kaunda on Violence*, he expressed his personal dilemma over how to obey the standard of Christ's cross, while directing the public machinery that is, often, necessarily brutal.

As for his senior colleagues, Kaunda declared, on the eve of the election, that during his next term no one would be exempt from the nation's leadership code - which was established to prevent corruption and conflict of interests among the nation's leaders - and which, thus far, has not really been effective.

But, in the election itself, the electorate chose to see the man as he had been officially drawn. He did not exactly kiss babies while campaigning, but one of his most visible posters had him holding a young child - who declares that she needs his help: he, meanwhile, needs your vote.

Two elections were held concurrently: for President and for Parliament. Separate polling slips were placed in separate polling boxes. For Parliament there was a broad choice of candidates. For President there was a single candidate.

If you approved of the President retaining office, you marked the square opposite 'Yes' and the Zambian eagle; if you did not approve, you marked the square opposite 'No' and a picture of a frog. As Lusaka wits described it, when you have a choice between Kenneth and Kermit, Kenneth has to win.

Many, however, expected Kermit to run him closer than he did. During Kaunda's last term, the war in Rhodesia had ended, but this did not lead to an improvement in Zambian living conditions.

He had faced, and overcome, a coup attempt; stared down a bitter protest from the Copperbelt miners; watched the price of copper fall on the world market; and lifted subsidies on food and basic commodities - largely in response to IMF pressure.

As early as 1980, *The Wall Street Journal* noted that in terms that had been adjusted for inflation, per capita income had dropped 14 per cent since 1970, exports had dropped 25 per cent since 1974, and consumer prices had risen 70 per cent. 'As a result, Mr. Kaunda . . . is facing the first serious opposition of his reign.'

At the same time, the *Financial Times* noted that 'the catalogue of mismanagement and of ill- conceived or badly implemented policies remains formidable.'

Many of Zambia's problems are structural ones, at the mercy more of world trends than local mismanagement. And, frankly, in terms of management, the country is doing well - considering that there were 99 black graduates on hand at independence.

But, to the common person, living is a more difficult achievement. Would he or she believe the explanations of international recession and poor terms of trade? And would he or she then believe that Kaunda was the only rock on which the nation could wait out these international storms and tides?

One of the popular stories of the campaign was of a parliamentary candidate who had been asked to speak for 15 minutes on the subject of international economic forces. After five minutes, he declared that someone had cast a spell on him, as his mouth could no longer speak on the subject.

Of course, the poor man had probably exhausted his knowledge of the intricacies of the world - far removed from the Lusaka compounds and squatter settlements. But, if aspiring MPs could not readily explain the international causes of Zambia's problems, could the electorate understand them? Privately, pundits were forecasting a 'No' vote of 40 per cent.

How then, in a continent often associated with rigged ballots, did Kaunda achieve such an emphatic endorsement? Firstly, it should be pointed out that he scored 93 per cent of the votes cast; that is 1,422,962 out of 1,529,016. But there were 2.4 million registered voters; so about one million abstained from voting, either from apathy or protest.

Secondly, the ruling UNIP Party had mounted an extremely competent campaign of "voter education". In UNIP's terms this meant educating the voters on how to vote 'Yes'. Certainly there was no countervailing campaign for a 'No' vote and, while such a campaign would not have been illegal, it would not have escaped harassment by UNIP 'militants'.

Thirdly, of course, there was no alternative candidate: a 'No' vote meant a vote for a vacuum as much as an expression of protest or dissatisfaction, and Kaunda is still widely regarded as a sincere man, though hardly a perfect one. The certainty of his remaining in power was preferable to the uncertainties of his departure.

Even so, the margin of his victory surprised many. Nor is there any evidence of ballot rigging - despite pre-election rumours that the many mock ballots being held as part of UNIP's voter education programme were identical to the official ballots and were to be stuffed into the official boxes if things looked like going wrong.

As there is no way such an exercise could be carried out nationally (the votes are counted locally) without a very great number of people being privy to it, with the normal risk of 'leaks', these rumours amount to no more than the usual electioneering scandal - mongering.

In any case, the total number of votes cast, constituency by constituency, as compared for the Presidential race and the Parliamentary race, tally quite nicely. Again the logistics of ballot - stuffing, with such a degree of precision, suggest that it did not happen. So, the result was surprising, but not unreasonable; and there have been no serious accusations of dishonesty.

Of greater interest, in terms of dissatisfaction with the ruling elite, were the Parliamentary elections. Primaries, which were a feature of previous elections, were dispensed with this time. Candidates were subject to UNIP scrutiny and endorsement, but only 46 out of 828 applicants were rejected.

These were, in the main, 'fringe' candidates who were unable to attract the Party's sense of humour. No real attempt was made to prevent real or imagined opponents to the Party from standing; each candidate had to hold a Party card of course, but among them were veterans of the 1976 university protest movement - apparently accepted as candidates without great difficulty.

The thought was that, perhaps, a crowded field would split any protest vote and allow incumbents to retain their seats. This is an unrealistic analysis; many sitting MPs are rather proud to be thorns in the side of the government and, while they are warned from time to time not to act excessively, a quasi-tradition of parliamentary protest has grown up-something definitely unusual in a one-party state.

In the event, no Cabinet Ministers lost their seats, several former Ministers and reasonably senior Party functionaries lost in their attempts to enter or re-enter Parliament, and several rather colourful MPs - many with the cloud of suspected corruption hanging over them - were defeated.

The campaign was largely free from violence, and all the official campaign speeches were made under Party programmes; all candidates were required to appear together, speak on the same topic, and refrain from putting up personal hoardings or posters.

This attempt to accord equal campaigning opportunities to rich and poor candidates alike also, naturally, ensures that no significant deviations are made from Party lines. Nevertheless, the campaign was not without colour, and much was made of the symbols chosen by the candidates to represent themselves to a not totally literate public.

Candidates who had chosen axes as symbols vowed to decapitate candidates who had chosen hens or roosters. If candidates occasionally messed up their lines about international economics, they tended to make up for it in traditional put-downs of their opponents, and in the humorous cut-and-thrust of campaign debate.

If the campaign was, thus, authentic, it did not really say too much about the national opinion of Zambia's mounting problems. Candidates were chiefly judged on their ability to deliver the goods locally: a bus route here, electricity there, more clinics, more schools.

Whether this suggests an electorate not sophisticated enough to understand the national and international issues at stake, or sophisticated enough to appreciate that their vote could not be structured to provide sufficient commentary on these issues, is open to question.

But there is some evidence to suggest that the average Zambian voter is no fool, but he or she is extremely pragmatic and willing to accept small or even token victories. An MP removed here or there will encourage the others.

At the start of the campaign, President Kaunda said that he had no interest in a life-presidency, even though it had been suggested often to him. After the elections, however, the *Times of Zambia* said in its editorial that it might not be necessary to subject the President to so many elections; he had won them all and was the "epitome of Zambia".

Clearly a kite is being flown here, but the amusement and superiority with which Zambians have lorded it over their Malawian counterparts - with their Life-President Dr. Banda - suggests that the kite may not fly high. Even so, Kaunda does stand at the centre of a small group of real power-holders - veterans of the independence movement.

With the death of Harry Nkumbula, Kaunda's only conceivable rival - and that only because of Nkumbula's historical prestige, not his actual capacities; for he died shortly before the elections, a broken and poverty-stricken man - the President has no perceivable rival.

Around Kaunda and his tight grouping, is a larger ill-defined collection, including some opportunists, and of course men and women of considerable ability. But it is an essentially small collection in the midst of the greater Zambian population.

This is not to deny the vast extent of Party influence and organisation throughout Zambia; but those who pull the levers, and who depend upon Kaunda for this privilege and the associated privileges of power, may well wish to press upon him the attractions of a life-presidency.

Whether this will be the case or not, the election signals no real policy changes for Zambia. Room for manoeuvre, in any case, is severely restricted: the price of copper is not rising, and the IMF conditions will definitely mean greater difficulties for the majority of Zambians.

The thorny questions of how best to manage what Zambia does have is still there. The ruling Party both suspects the growing crop of Zambians with PhDs, and continues to entice them away from the university to direct the growing state apparatus. A common lecturer can find himself, overnight, with the salary of a Permanent Secretary, and in charge of a vast operation with little real chance of success.

For Zambia has developed a comprehensive apparatus. There is even a modest social security scheme. Everything is in place, ready to spring into action - ready to contribute to the nation at some future 'take-off' point. But the date for take-off seems to recede. It is not always that policies are ill-conceived, but that there is no money to implement policies.

As for the institutions of life which mark a nation as liberal and democratic, Zambia continues to garner reasonably high marks. And, in his swearing-in for a fifth term, Kaunda - as well as warning the new crop of MPs not to get too uppity - promised to respect the judiciary and the freedom of the press.

As for his massive majority, the President said that he would look to God for guidance. ''Your love frightens me. I do not know how I can measure up to the desires and wishes of the Zambian people."

In what seemed to be a carefully staged, or fortuitously timed interview with *Africa Now* - one of the few international magazines available in Zambia - Kaunda was given free rein to portray himself as a sensitive, Christian, liberal democrat. He appeared, by turns, shy and assertive - in short, charming and impressive in what is now a well - practiced, almost stereotyped fashion.

The interviewer, Peter Enahoro, was clearly impressed - though naturally suspicious of charming politicians. Describing Kaunda's contradictions, Enahoro concluded, "perhaps in their sum total the contradictions demonstrate the character of an idealist who has learned from experience that politics is the art of the possible".

Those few things that are immediately possible for Zambia may still be forthcoming only after God's help. The next five years will be hard for the President and Zambia. The signal of the smooth election, and its singular result, might well be that the Zambian people are cautiously digging in deep for the lean times ahead.

ZAMBIA'S FOREIGN POLICY - ELITISM AND POWER (1984)

Zambia's Foreign Policy has always been reactive. The country's location and the regional pressures of the last 20 years have conditioned a foreign policy that has appeared vague, contradictory, tailored to benefit a Zambian elite, or simply naive. In any case, the cold war between the superpowers, Zambia's nearness to South Africa, UDI in Rhodesia shortly after Zambia's independence, the problem of Zambia's transport links, and the effect these have on her export capacities and import requirements, have constituted a phalanx of pressures that the country, sometimes boldly, sometimes with great meekness, has reacted to - there have been few initiatives in foreign policy, in which Zambia has laid down the ground rules for another's reaction.

To a significant extent, Zambia's lack of professional personnel at independence is still reflected in the absence of any real professional base in her foreign service. Foreign policy formation and important diplomatic movements have been conducted on a political level, with little professional input. With the exception of a handful of names, such as Vernon Mwaanga and Mark Chona, foreign policy formation has been closely identified with the President and, often, with the President alone. The country that had a total of 99 graduates at independence still does not have a cadre of graduate diplomats in the core of her foreign service.

With independence, of course, came the natural desire to be seen as a state with appropriate international trappings. Embassies were opened and received. Elaborately, the motions were gone through and particularly, with the ceremonial visits of foreign heads of state, the country felt confirmed in her place among other independent states. These diplomatic forms have what Adam Watson calls `the value of status symbols'. (1) African heads of state regularly appear to visit one another, conferring, or exchanging, tokens of status as they do so. The East

European countries, aware of the value of diplomatic forms, have regularly dispatched presidential or high - level ministerial delegations to African nations, and have won superficial but accumulated points for doing so.

Distinct stages in the superpower rivalry

The interest of the eastern bloc in Africa has not been confined to the conferment of status. Although Stalin had been deeply suspicious of African nationalist leaders, viewing them as 'bourgeois imperialist lackeys', divorced from their proletariats upon whom revolution depended, Khrushchev saw them as leaders of nations that could be induced to forsake the west. In his logic, a loss for the west was necessarily a gain for the east. This logic ignored any intermediate categories such as non-alignment, and set the tone for much of the superpower rivalry that followed. Khrushchev devoted large sums in economic and military aid to African countries, particularly those with ostensibly progressive regimes - Nkrumah's Ghana, Keita's Mali, Toure's Guinea, Ben Bella's Algeria, Nasser's Egypt - and set about convincing the African states that, by contrast, the USA was uninterested in African development. By the time of Brezhnev's administration, the unreliability of African progressivism was apparent; sudden changes of regime could undermine years of investment. Soviet aid was henceforth to be conditioned by stricter criteria, and by the US response to the Khrushchev largesse. The strategic importance of the country concerned, its economic importance as a market for Soviet exports or a provider of raw materials, and the importance of western bloc influence in the region, formed the new criteria for aid. (2)

What had been the US response to the Khrushchev largesse? The Kennedy administration had noted the Soviet interest in Africa, but did not try to match the volume of Soviet aid. However, the USA could not appear as uninterested in African development as the Soviets had depicted them; moreover, using Soviet logic, the USA could not allow new nations, overnight, to be lost to the west. Kennedy's rhetorical gifts, which had carried him so far at home, were now applied to an audience of African leaders. Comparing the drive for civil rights in the USA to the African urge to secure justice in South Africa, Kennedy gave the impression of a genuine US interest in African affairs; and, to a large extent, the African nations took the rhetoric for policy.(3) Nothing of substance ever came of the rhetoric, but the African leaders seemed to believe it - so much so that Babu accused Nkrumah himself of establishing a ''diplomatic tradition in Africa of playing off the US against Europe with the argument that only the US could exert pressure on Europe to free the rest of Africa''. (4) According to Babu, faced with a historic choice between the forces of socialism and capitalism, Africa succumbed to the blandishments of capitalism.

Having so cheaply blunted the Soviet initiative, the US view of Africa did not appear to increase in complexity. When, by the first Nixon administration, the National Security Council Interdepartmental Group for Africa was asked to assess US prospects in Southern Africa, its findings, completed by August 1969, were both narrowly based and amazingly wide of the mark. (5) Liberation movements were deemed unable, in the foreseeable future, to overthrow or seriously threaten white regimes in Angola, Mozambique, Rhodesia, Namibia, or South Africa - the conclusions on the two Portuguese colonies being made without any reference to possible changes within Portugal. Two remarks are of particular interest to the present essay: "The Soviets appear to afford Africa a low priority at present and can be expected to limit the extent of their commitment and involvement." (6) "Zambia shows latent instability for tribal reasons, and may face internal crisis" (7). The second of these two remarks will be considered in due course. The first remark couches the future of US policy towards Southern Africa in terms of Soviet activity in the area. The implication was that so long as the Soviets stayed out, there was no real point in the USA going in. The USA had no inherent interest in Africa, unless first the Soviet Union demonstrated its interest.

For the Soviets, meantime, their view of Africa was being complicated by the rise of Chinese interest in the continent. The Chinese had singularly championed a species of non-alignment - China and the Third World separate and against the USA and the Soviet Union - which had its roots in the Bandung Conference of 1955, and was first specifically applied to Africa 10 years later when Zhou Enlai attempted, abortively, to replicate the Bandung Conference in Algiers, and establish an international alliance which excluded the superpowers. (8) Following (ironically) the Khrushchev strategy of large-scale aid, the Chinese have, averaged out, spent $100 million in each country; much of the time justifying their outlay by reference to the (now defunct) Three Worlds Theory. (9)

It was in Angola that the US, Soviet, Chinese, South African, and Zambian foreign policies found a specific theatre in which confrontation with one another seemed inevitable.

Moderation on all her borders and moderation within.

To a large extent, Angola was a testing ground for the foreign policy approaches of the five countries mentioned above. For the first four countries, it provided an experimental model in how far close support of one faction, or actual intervention on behalf of one faction, could direct the course of events in a large area of Africa. Adrian Guelke has outlined the fluid circumstances surrounding the birth of Angola that each of our powers tried to make flow to its advantage. (10) There are, of course, various views on the motivation of the powers involved in Angola. Ogunbadejo maintains that the MPLA always looked likely to win the struggle for government, and that the Soviet Union did not intervene, with the help of Cuba, until after the western powers, with South Africa clearly in the lead, attempted to change what had previously seemed the *status quo*. (11) The Chinese intervened because the Soviets intervened against the western intervention, etc.. This is an interesting new version of the domino theory: one intervention leads to another. It is not strictly accurate - circumstances were very fluid - but provides an impressionistic view of Africa's place in the foreign policies of others: either neutral interest in the continent, or the need to neutralize the interest of others. In short, the need is for ascertainable governments - governments that are predictable, that operate within internationally recognized frameworks, that do not destabilize their region, that are moderate fixtures in a continent regarded as immoderate due to its unpredictability. Perhaps to make plain a complicated continent, the powers have first imputed then tried to foster particular roles for particular countries. What now concerns this essay is how far Zambia has adopted a similar foreign policy towards its neighbours.

If, however, Zambia's foreign policy has always been reactive, in what context has she conducted her foreign policy? To many, her foreign policy has often appeared contradictory. The authors of the preface to one of Timothy Shaw's works pointed out the apparent inconsistency between a President Kaunda who, in his 1975 visit to the USA, appealed for US support for African efforts to achieve majority rule in Rhodesia and Namibia; and the Zambian foreign policy that supported, in Angola, the UNITA/FNLA coalition alongside the USA and South Africa. Although Shaw himself did not make so specific a charge-of collusion between Zambian policymakers and outside forces over Angola - he did generally point out the `clear coincidence' of elite Zambian interests and external interests, (12) and thus advocated a point of view which proceeds from a critical linkage between elite class privileges and the formation of foreign policy to advance or preserve these privileges. This is part of a broader international analysis, in which "internal inequalities are related to international stratification". (13) As far as Zambian foreign policy is concerned, this school of thought has offered a persistent and influential critique - advanced in works by Shaw, but also by many others. (14) Applying this critique to Angola, it would have seemed necessary at least to suspect the collusion of elite Zambian and South African interests. That is to say, Zambian foreign policy is conducted in the context of South African foreign policy; there is an overlap of interests between the two policymaking groups, based not only on regional perceptions but on the privileges such a coincidence confers.

Not so, says William Tordoff. Replying directly to Shaw, Tordoff maintains that "such arguments give insufficient weight to the intense nationalism of Zambia's leadership' and her overall record of support for liberation struggles". (15) Tordoff places Zambian foreign policy very much in a national context of change - change that sought to end external domination - rather than in international context in which domination, and collusion with domination, are the key factors. The events leading up to the Angolan situation, Tordoff says, were marked by Zambian disengagement from the Westminster style of parliamentary democracy, i.e. entering the Second Republic with its single party system; disengagement from external ideologies, both western and eastern; in favour of humanism; and the attempt, largely through seeking alternative transport links, to disengage from the South African-dominated regional economic system.

There is great merit in both the Shaw and Tordoff approaches, and it might be of benefit to examine whether the two might be more easily combined than it first appears. Tordoff admits that, during this period, many mistakes were made in Zambian foreign policy, e.g. encouraging Nkomo to talk to Smith as late as December 1975, when guerilla war seemed the only means of liberation; and siding with UNITA in the Angolan war. Furthermore, Tordoff states that the foreign policy strategy which perpetrated such mistakes was based on "compromising contact with South Africa". (16) Moreover, Douglas Anglin has written that Zambia's position was that the `attitude of the western powers was crucial' to her plans during the early stages of her support for the liberation struggle in Rhodesia. (17) All this tends to indicate a foreign policy which recognized certain limits, particularly limits imposed by other powers. Depending on one's point of view, this is either a realistic or a collaborative regimen. But there were also other factors in play, as Anglin points out. For instance, Zambia has always tried to unite the disparate Zimbabwe guerilla groups, ZANU and ZAPU, and also, in Angola, the MPLA and FLNA - but to no final avail. (18) That is, Zambia has preached unity to the freedom groups as a *sine qua non* for success. Alongside guerilla unity, another major Zambian diplomatic effort was towards, as far as possible, the peaceful settlement of regional disputes. Hence, President Kaunda's Special Assistant for Foreign Affairs, Mark Chona, engaged in much shuttle diplomacy between Lisbon and Frelimo, attempting to establish a peaceful transition of power in Mozambique. His was a critical intervention, helping to prevent an Angolan-type situation. Chona was also involved in, for a time, a pretty constant shuttle among Pretoria, Salisbury, London, ZANU, ZAPU, and Lusaka, attempting to establish a common basis for negotiation. In short, whether or not the cloud of South African power hung over the region, and over Zambian foreign policy, that foreign policy nonetheless sought to establish, in Zambian terms, a humanist context for the solution of regional problems.

While conceding this, it would be unwise to take it all at face value. Underlying this humanist approach was a deep Zambian conservatism: the problems of the region needed to be solved; they needed resolution in a manner which Zambia, caught in the middle of them all, could predict, if not control. If South Africa had exactly the same view, then the foreign policies of the two countries did, at this point, indeed coincide. As Shaw says, both countries saw the solution to the Rhodesian problem as a Zimbabwe acceptable to both Zambia and South Africa. That is, a Zimbabwe won, not by guerilla war, but by negotiation - with the compromises that entails. Thus, Zambia encouraged Nkomo to parlay with Smith in 1975. Shaw says that the search for a peaceful solution was compatible with the elite-guided reformism of humanism, and consistent with Zambia's need to have secure transport links to the outside world.(19) This is consistent with Tordoff's three disengagements, except that Shaw continues to emphasize the critical role of Zambia's elite.

On Tordoff's first disengagement, from the Westminster style of democracy, this has been propounded, within Zambia as a need to consolidate national unity, i.e. unity is wrought through a one- party state. There was a significant build up to the Second Republic. Writing before its announcement, Jan Pettman, described at length President Kaunda's emphasis on the need for national unity (20). Taken at face value, it all seemed persuasive; except, as Graham Mytton pointed out, in a review of Pettman's book (written with the hindsight of the proclamation of the Second Republic), it could also be interpreted as a case in which a privileged elite found means to preserve and extend itself. (21) Or, perhaps, as a means whereby policymakers could render their society more governable and predictable. The coincidence of the stress on unity, both internally, and in the approaches of freedom groups in other countries, suggest a search for moderation within Zambia, and on her borders. How far is it also a reflection of an elite's strategy to maintain its internal ascendancy by tailoring foreign policy?

Perhaps one suspects an elite domination of internal Zambian policy, but questions whether this domination also applies to foreign policy. It is well to be reminded, at this stage, of the National Security Council's view that Zambia was showing 'latent instability for tribal reasons, and may face internal crises'. One may perhaps then suspect elite domination of internal Zambian policy but concede good reasons for its drive for national unity. Whether or not this is indeed the case is properly the subject of a separate enquiry; but, in terms of a domination of foreign policy, in order to preserve class privileges, the case for elite domination is a weak one.

First, as noted at the beginning of this essay, there is no professional basis for the conduct of foreign policy. There is no influential foreign service, no influential academics or journalists who specialize in international affairs. In the realm of political diplomacy, the dominant figure is that of the President, not that of a discernible class. There are no foreign policy think-tanks or publications. In short, there are none of the characteristics associated with a foreign policy establishment. There is, therefore, no apparatus by which any group of people can influence or dominate foreign policy formation.

Second, if one extends the argument and locates elite domination of foreign policy primarily in economic foreign policy, and indicates the sprawling apparatus of para-statals, and also the small private commercial sector, as an apparatus for dominating foreign policy, one is still on insecure ground. It is true that the para-statals behave in capitalist terms, and also true that most of them depend on foreign exchange in order to function properly. But there is no evidence that, together, or even singly, they have sought to collude with international capitalist forces, to determine structurally the nation's foreign policy in order to secure the nation's meagre foreign exchange. Even if they did so, there would still be the argument as to whether it was done to maintain or improve the capacities of the para-statals, or to benefit the class that runs them. As it is, questions of international economic consequence are not made by the para-statals. The evidence suggests very much that State House determines such questions: some para-statals flourish accordingly; others decline; the managerial class involved continues to draw its benefits as a result of the employment of its members, not whether their companies are successful.

Third, if one narrows elite domination of foreign policy, not only to economic foreign policy, but to the single half-viable economic instrument available to Zambia, that is copper, one still has no evidence to sustain the proposition. The factors mentioned in the last paragraph apply also to the copper industry. Even if they did not, one is here talking of an extremely narrow elite; and, in Zambia, one best noted for its technocratic skills rather than its avarice.

Fourth, in other African countries, without a network of para-statals and without mineral wealth, there are still elites who may be thought to dominate policy formation. The economic apparatus of Zambia does not necessarily double as an apparatus for foreign policy formation. If one maintains that, outside apparatus, elite domination is informal, and the benefits of domination are generally diffused to the elite, one then has no way of measuring and proving the matter.

Objective external factors: the case of transport links.

It might be beneficial to examine some well-documented pressures on Zambian foreign policy. Zambia is a landlocked country; as such, its dependency on other nations for the maintenance of transport routes, and its vulnerability to foreign policy changes by its neighbours, are constant factors. (22) Zambia entered independence and, shortly thereafter, confronted Rhodesian UDI on her southern border; having, as a colonial inheritance, a concentration of railway routes pointing south, and a history of political confusion in the region over pointing railways in any other direction. (23) The Zambian response to UDI was to search, at times frantically, for possibilities of routes elsewhere. The TANZAM railway was one result of this search. Zambia became ``a nub of a network of strategic highways". Since Zambia's economy depended upon "getting the copper out, so have her politics centred upon the overriding question of communication". (24)

To an extent, this search for other rail routes was evidence of Tordoff's third disengagement, with which Shaw also concurs. Except that it was never a search simply for non-southern routes. Smith did close the border in 1973. But, at the 1975 Victoria Falls conference, Vorster offered to act as guarantor that Smith would reopen the border for a free-flow of rail traffic. Then, Kaunda refused to cooperate; but did so three years later, in 1978, and a transport agreement was signed between the South African and Zambian railways (i.e. an agreement between technical, not political, bodies). (25) Why did Zambia not agree to open her border for rail traffic in 1975, but did so in 1978 - when Rhodesia was still under UDI? Geldenhuys provides a fascinating account from Vorster of the 1975 conference. According to this, Kaunda could not open the border because this would jeopardize Zambia's standing among the front-line states -particularly with Tanzania. (26) By 1978, however, Zambia had the benefit of alternative transport routes. The southern border could be opened, and dialogue with the South Africans take place, without a total dependence on South African pressure on Rhodesia to keep the southern route open. The search had been for transport routes free from political jeopardy. It was not a disengagement from South African economic domination, but an attempt to meet it from slightly stronger ground. If this was the case, we can perceive a degree of sophistication in the Zambian foreign policy response to South African pressure. (27)

The view from South Africa.

How does South Africa view its neighbours? Even on what appears to be a clear-cut issue such as Namibia, Geldenhuys suggests that South Africa's true intentions are not easily discerned. (28) What is, by now, a pretty standard analysis has been advanced by Robert M. Price. South African foreign policy is divided into three: the long-term strategy is still towards the constellation of surrounding, dependent states; the medium-term strategy is towards the neutralization of troublesome neighbours; and the short-term strategy is to avoid western remonstrations by stressing the Soviet/Cuban presence in the region. (29)

Where does Zambia fit into this? In the long-term view, Zambia's championing of SADCC constitutes an attempt to establish what may be called a counter -

constellation. In the medium-term, there is no need for South Africa to 'neutralize' Zambia, as Zambia has never threatened South Africa; has always conducted her foreign policy with clear signals to Pretoria on the meeting and limits of statements; has highlighted her regional diplomacy by sudden bouts of political summitry with South Africa. In a sense, South Africa should be very pleased with Zambian foreign policy: it provides Pretoria with a sense of influence in a respected black state. Having said this, one should point out that this state of affairs is a long way from the collusion of a Zambian ruling class with South African interests; particularly as the view from Lusaka is probably that of Zambia as one of two poles of power in the region - the other being South Africa-and that Lusaka and Pretoria form a sort of balance, without which the black independent states of the region would be much worse off. Maintaining the balance means two things: firstly, Zambia must concede a range of initiatives to South Africa - since South Africa is the more powerful pole; second, the diplomatic intercourse between the two concerns the nature of a region that both Lusaka and Pretoria can live with. If, from Pretoria's viewpoint, this hinges on a constellation of dependent states, then, from Lusaka's viewpoint, the aim of Zambian foreign policy is to diminish this dependency until it is something that underlies rather than overshadows the region. From both points of view, it seems a game worth playing.

Elements of a pole of power.

In terms of the normal factors of power, such as those advanced by Morgenthau; or, in terms of resources to deploy power in specific situations over specific actors, thus wielding power in the sense meant by Baldwin and Hart; Zambia's power capacity is considerably less than South Africa's. Rather than seeking to match South Africa's power in any conventional sense, Zambia has sought to seem powerful through amassing influence. Here, the role of humanism is a major one - not as a touchstone for elite - guided reformism, as seen by Shaw, but as embodied in the Zambian President in his political diplomacy. Rather than foreign policy being tailored by an internal Zambian elite, foreign policy is designed to propose Zambia as an elite nation in a troubled region. The amassing of influence takes place as follows:

1) The image of moral suasion, as embodied in a humanist president, by precedent and protestation concerned with dialogue and arbitration - among both allies and antagonists.

2) The Zambian role in international groupings. Not groupings of a conventional sort such as the UN; but groupings which emphasize summitry among heads of state and government - such as the OAU, the Non-Aligned Movement, and the Commonwealth - again, so that a national image may be personified. (30)

3) The image of predictability. Zambia is portrayed relentlessly as a unified nation and, thereby, stable. Its government is consistent, persistent, and may be counted upon.

4) The image of potential alliance. Although non-aligned, Zambia has always let it be known that she values her relationships with western nations; demanding, in turn, to be informed, if not consulted, by western powers on southern African issues.

5) The chaperone image, or the image of older brother, elder statesman, by which it is considered that Zambia can control liberation groups stationed on her territory, and condition the approach of their leaders. To a lesser extent, this image persists when viewing Zambia in the context of the frontline states.

These images of Zambia and the Zambian President cannot be projected on behalf of any other black southern African state. Zambian foreign policy is always swift to portray Lusaka as an international centre: it was where the SADCC plan of action was drawn up; it was where the Commonwealth achieved its breakthrough over Rhodesia. Sometimes, the assiduous political diplomacy of it all is seen to go astray - as in the meetings of parties to the Namibian dispute in Lusaka in the first part of 1984. Although in keeping with President Kaunda's penchant for arbitration, and his belief in the powers of his personal moral suasion (he was in the chair for 20 hours at one session), the conference of delegates from SWAPO, the internal parties, South Africa, with the South African Administrator-General periodically in the chair, was nothing more than a propaganda triumph for Pretoria. Less bizarre has been Zambia's approach to SADCC and the regional PTA. Here, the prospect is of a counter - constellation (if it actually constellates) dominated by Zimbabwean economic clout. Lusaka cannot afford to let Harare grow into the regional capital. If it does so, Zambian influence will be diminished. When, eventually, SADCC grows sufficiently to warrant a secretariat, the comings and goings as to where it should be sited will be interesting. In the meantime, the practice of a diffused administration, shared among the various national civil services, postpones this debate. (31)

There are some current manifestations of rivalry, both somewhat against the essential spirit of SADCC: Zimbabwe has been given the SADCC portfolio for aviation training, but there is a fully operational aviation school in Lusaka; there is a large veterinary school in Harare, with sufficient capacity to serve the region, but the Zambians are delighted to see being built for them, by the Japanese, a replica of one of the largest Japanese veterinary schools.

Nevertheless, because in overall terms Zambia has developed various characteristics of influence, and tries hard to give the impression that, through its influence, it can mobilize powerful friends, she is the region's only candidate for the foreseeable future for the role of counterweight to South Africa. It is, necessarily, a defensive role: South Africa takes the lead and Zambia responds. This realization and strategy lies at the heart of Zambia's foreign policy.

Two points can be made in summary. First, it is the contention of this essay that Zambian foreign policy is in the hands of the President and is not selfishly dominated by an elite class. Second, the aim of Zambian foreign policy is not to disengage from South Africa's sphere of influence, but to act as its regional counterweight. This allows dealings with South Africa: there is no question of boycotting South African facilities; there is a question of avoiding absolute dependence on them. Although there are overlaps in the Shaw and Tordoff analyses, both miss these essential points.

On this basis, one can make an interesting projection for SADCC. The more SADCC grows, the freer Zambia will feel to trade with South Africa. That is, the growth of SADCC will be seen as providing a basis whereby trade with South Africa will not be fraught with dependency to the extent that Zambia feels herself in political jeopardy. Constellation or counter-constellation, there is no naive thought of actual disengagement, but thought to control the overlap between two regional poles.

If, within SADCC, there is no true aim of self - sufficiency, neither in Zambia is there any capacity to develop economic self-sufficiency outside it. Notwithstanding depressing international economic conditions, the parlous state of the Zambian economy is not helped by the poor efforts of its representatives in international economic diplomacy - this being very much a result of an unprofessional diplomatic cadre.

Perhaps economic conditions will encourage closer links with western financial interests. These have always been associated with the country, and do not indicate also a political dependency on western powers. The west does, however, appear to be regarded as an open-ended fashion from Lusaka - whereas the eastern bloc is firmly circumscribed. The west can deliver, in the southern African region, what the east cannot: that is, pressure towards independence for Namibia; and pressure towards reforms inside South Africa. To resist the west, South Africa uses the threat of the east, i.e. the Soviet/Cuban presence in Angola. Zambia seeks to encourage the west in its pressure, and has always done so in the region's liberation struggles. The west, particularly the USA, is seen as an object within Zambian regional policy; Zambia does not regard herself as an agent in US policy.

Can this sort of performance, involving much adroit movement to stay on line, continue after Kaunda? Perhaps then, the well-noted Zambian penchant for material comfort will lead to closer links with South Africa - beyond that afforded from a position of (tenuous but nevertheless apparent) strength. Perhaps that will come.

But, until then, the day of an elite domination of Zambian foreign policy for its own economic class interests has not yet dawned.

HUMANISM, INTELLECTUALS AND THE LEFT IN ZAMBIA (1984)

Zambia became independent in 1964, adopted humanism as its national philosophy in 1967, and became a one- party state in 1972. Kenneth Kaunda has been the nation's only president. He is the head of state, commander-in-chief of the armed forces, and has vested in his office the executive powers of the republic. Under these conditions there has not really been the development of a Zambian intellectual history. In this paper, I shall attempt to describe the faint outline of intellectual movements discernible in Zambia, and provide a structure by which the substance of intellectual development may be viewed over the next twenty years.

A caveat to start with: we are dealing here with intellectual development as it relates to the working of the Zambian state; we are not suggesting that the nation's cultural history is bereft of intellectual merit; but the Zambian state celebrates, this year, only its twentieth anniversary - so our perspective is contemporary and deals with the institutions of government that are themselves modern and modernising. To what extent has intellectual development influenced the development of the state?

The British had colonised Africa in such a way that, on the west coast, educational provision for the indigenous population extended as far as university education. In east Africa and what was then Northern Rhodesia, the emphasis was on primary education --- the white settler population was greater in the east; it required skilled labour; this meant that primary education was viewed as an important service to the white management of the eastern countries, but anything higher was deemed superfluous, if not dangerous. When Zambia attained independence, therefore, there existed a total of 99 Zambian university graduates. Very few of these had received their education by virtue of official British foresight, but had attracted the support of private charities, private scholarships, or had attended the universities of other developing countries - themselves newly independent - like India. Both the current Zambian Prime Minister, Namulimo Mundia, and his predecessor, Daniel Lisulo, studied in India; but they were among a very small minority of those who campaigned for independence. For the most part, the African intellectuals of the day were regarded as intellectuals by virtue of being teachers or clerks. Kaunda, himself, had been a teacher.

Even so, these people were much influenced by trends in political thought overseas. The concept of a centralised state provision of essential services owes more, in Zambia, to the work of Harold Laski than a distant appreciation of the Soviet model. The founders of the Zambian state worked to create a replica of the social democracy they had read about. Even in its most strident enunciation, it has never been regarded as a fully - formed socialism - although the term `socialism' is a rhetorical commonplace. But, as far as resources would allow, the aim was to create an African welfare state. It remains one of the few black African states with a social welfare system - although this functions on an extremely modest footing. The Zambian housing schemes for rural migrants to the cities were models both of compassion and sensible planning to the rest of Africa; and the current efforts to install a functioning primary health care programme again place Zambia in the forefront of African effort in social development - a paradigm of latest thought in health care, materialising from World Health Organisation treatises, and being established in the rural infra - structure by Zambian effort.

One of the priorities of the independent government was to fill the vacuum that existed in place of higher education. The University of Zambia was established in 1965, and received its first Zambian Vice-Chancellor in 1969. The university has been closed four times because of student unrest; occasionally expatriate lecturers are expelled as undesirable influences; but the steadily growing core of Zambian academics has never really been controversial. They take their place, in the international mould of liberal (but silent) academics, in a state that is ostensibly liberal. If one were to consider the five basic institutional freedoms - freedom of the judiciary, of the press, of the churches, of the trade unions, and of the university - then Zambia is certainly a liberal third world country. An ostensible state of affairs, however, is not necessarily a real one. It would be well to examine the setting in which academics, and other Zambian intellectuals, find themselves.

City-Based Development

Zambia is the most urbanised black African nation: 40% of the population resides in cities and towns; it is expected that this will increase to 50% by the year 2000. It might seem that Zambia provides a classic example of the dual economy usually associated with third world countries: that is, a small, heavily subscribed `export enclave' attracts development funding, with its export-oriented products either manufactured or processed in cities; while, in the rural areas, the mass of the population subsists - much as it has done from time immemorial, untouched by the benefits of development, except to be made bitter that such benefits are beyond their reach.

In the case of Zambia, the notion of a dual economy is itself merely nostalgic. The nation has always depended upon the export of copper-which earns Zambia 94% of its foreign exchange, while another mineral, cobalt, earns about 3%. The rural economy, which is meant to centre itself around agriculture, is depressed to the extent that agricultural production depends upon large-scale commercial holdings and equally-large state farms. In terms of volume of production, the small-scale farmer and peasant doesn't really feature. Of course, agricultural production is geared to feed the cities - so what we have is, in fact, a single, export-oriented economy, with a tiny and depressed rural subsistence enclave.

The increase in urban population, therefore, merely mirrors the trend of economic development. Those who have trekked to the cities have, until recently at least, come under the provenance of model housing schemes. What that term means in reality is that Zambian cities are surrounded by a higher class of shanty than in other parts of Africa; but, if one were to define a slum in terms of what exists in Lagos, or in terms of the Mathare Valley in Nairobi, there are no real slums in Zambia. It is the benefits of urban life that accord Zambia one of the highest per capita incomes in Africa: comparable to the rich neighbour, Zimbabwe. Urban concentration, and enlightened policies accompanying this, have meant a fairer distribution of wealth. In countries with larger rural populations, distribution of wealth is firmly biased in favour of the small urban populations. In Zambia, the massive urban population ensures a greater economic equity. So much so that Zambia is classed with Algeria in the table of the world's middle-income countries. And there are certainly more schools and clinics than in most other African countries.

The question of clinics is an interesting one. It seems that the greater number of rural clinics is staffed by expatriate personnel, e.g. volunteer doctors or medics from the Indian sub-continent treading the first rung on the ladder to greener pastures; Zambian medical graduates attempt, as far as possible, to practice in the cities. Intellectual life is centered in the cities. The University of Zambia is an urban institution, so are the other major tertiary colleges. The seat of government, centre of all professions, headquarters of the trade unions, centre of the publishing houses, are in the cities.

Humanism and Power

Humanism is a social philosophy that owes its existence to Kenneth Kaunda. While it owes its propagation to the single party (the United National Independence Party), UNIP, this is because Kaunda is also the founder and the president of that party. Such is his command of the nation, and the genuine respect with which much of the nation holds him, that his personal formulation of how mankind should live has been adopted, officially, as the national philosophy, and everywhere lip-service is paid to it. It is difficult to see, however, how Humanism can outlive Kaunda. It is not a rigorous formulation: that is, it is neither an academic philosophy nor an ideology. It provides no theoretical base by which the world may be analysed, and from which action can spring. This deficiency, in particular, has made sceptics of the younger intellectual generation as we shall observe below. Humanism is, essentially, a series of axioms concerning the desirability of a man - centred society. It owes much to the rationalist and humanist movements of post-war Europe, and probably owes its idealism, indeed some of its early romanticism, to a superficial appreciation of existentialism - that is, the existentialism of a Camus, rather than Sartre.

Nor is Humanism a social philosophy concerned with the dynamics of human agency. It does not posit that man is the centre of history and that his actions condition the historical process. Rather, in speaking of a man-centred society, Humanism has come to mean that the political apparatus of society should have, as its first objective, the satisfaction of human needs, and should have, in its bureaucratic processes, a constant view of the human personality. Humanism's man-centred society is one where its centre, man, is provided for. In the name of history, nor under any other name, man does not seek to overturn his social condition - if that condition is the result of Humanism's provision.

Humanism is, therefore, simultaneously humane and conservative. Its humane aspects have been celebrated internationally, and Kaunda has acquired and maintained a distinct international personality of a most favourable sort. This has pleased observers of every stripe. Firstly, Kaunda's Humanism is propagated as being superior to humanism with a small 'h', since it combines that basically agnostic humanism with a strong and deliberate Christian character; secondly, the formulation that Humanism may be approached via socialism lends Humanism, and the Zambian state, a socialist aura; thirdly, and conversely, the primacy of Humanism over socialism means that every option is kept open, provided that these options accord with the generally liberal foundations of Humanist thought.

The conservatism of the national philosophy, however, has attracted less international attention. In part, this is because of the lack of any structured and sustained dissidence to Humanism - as, again, we shall discuss below. The conservatism has also been administered in a subtle manner. Here, we have the necessary corollary of Zambia as the most urbanised black African state; it is also the most thoroughly administered. Humanism exists to inform the actions of the party; the party exists to manage society, so that the font of Humanism, and the state apparatus which emanates from its position, may be protected. Throughout the urban shanties and housing estates - that is, throughout the third estate of Zambian urban life: beneath the elite and sub-elite - the party fields a most complex and far-reaching organisation. This organisation simultaneously represents the mass urban population, and regulates it. It is a national expression of self-censorship, and the primary device of state security, operating alongside the official security service - that is, the secret service - itself ably trained by the east Germans. Its far - reaching existence - no aspect of shanty life escapes its notice - means that the urban masses are politically compliant and operate through the UNIP structure as a given norm, in much the same way as, in the rural areas, operating through village elders is a given norm. None of this is viciously imposed. It is accepted, rather than imposed at all. For, despite having one of the highest per capita incomes in its region, Zambia's economy is, in the current international recession, balanced on a knife -edge. The extent of party control is a persuasive element in the minds of urban dwellers. Access to scarce commodities might be made more difficult if one did not tow the line. The end-result of the party presence is a formidable self-regulation among the population. This leaves dissidence to the elite and sub–elite - but there exist devices to control them too , though not as thoroughly.

The pervasive character of the party means that it can provide a complex career structure. This structure is constantly expanding - in part to reward greater numbers of party faithful. The exercise in governmental de-centralisation, introduced in the early 1980s, merely provided another level of party patronage. The centralised government structure remained much as it did before. To it was added an extensive appendage. No demonstrable increase in the rate of national development has accompanied this extension - although this was the public rationale for its introduction. This decentralisation was planned on the Tanzanian model. Embarrassingly, the Tanzanians repudiated this structure in their own country, just as it was being introduced to Zambia. It had not brought, to Tanzania, any additional development. In Zambia, its developmental worth is secondary: it allows another staging post for party control and management. Development and the benefits of government are the results of the state apparatus. As elsewhere, so in Zambia, the primary question of apparatus is who controls its power; the benefits emanating from the apparatus form a secondary concern, sometimes incidental.

Where does this leave the Kaunda of international repute? Surprisingly, the man has laid his cards on the table. His latest book, *Kaunda on Violence*, might be sub-titled, `Confessions of a Chastened Humanist'. It seems not to have been widely read, although it attracted a blistering review in *African Affairs*, the authoritative journal of the Royal Africa Society. In this book, Kaunda discourses on the contradiction between idealism and the realities of power. It is a most honest statement, but, of itself, does little to reinstate liberal values and expression as individual rights in Zambia.

Power and the International Recession

There is a very respectable school of thought that analyses Zambian society in terms of its division between a comprador class, aiding and abetting international capitalism for individual gain, and the mass of the people who are the victims of an international dependency and thus, at present, of the international recession. In some respects, this school of thought is related to that of the dual economy. Likewise, it has the same defect as the dual economy school - in that, while there may well be a comprador class (and this is not the place for a full discussion of that), the extremely large urban population is its collaborator, and hopes to be a beneficiary of this collaboration. In short, if there is a comprador class, it is a large one or, at least, one capable of an extended definition. Within what may best be called an urban class, there are three readily identifiable divisions, alluded to earlier, and common reference points to Zambian sociologists: elite, sub-elite, and shanty (or, as they are known in Zambia, compound) dwellers. All form parts of an urban society, knowingly and deliberately dependent on the mechanisms of international capitalism. The overall standard of living is such that all wish to preserve it, and do not want to take chances in actual, as opposed to rhetorical, changes of economic policy. Within this urban class, the three divisions do refer to major differences of wealth. In continental terms, these divisions are not extreme. While they are not within the much more narrow band that prevails in Tanzania, they are not so great as to ferment active and continuing resentment. Although the elite drive Mercedes limousines, their consumption is conspicuous mostly in private. That is, the elite is decorous to the extent that the poor merely envy them.

The division is not problematic because of its division between rich and poor. It is problematic in that there has occurred not only a polarisation of wealth, but what American sociologists call an aglutinization of values: that is, all the material values of society have been attracted to the same small group; the elite is not only rich, it is educated, and it holds political power.

The poor do not rebel against the rich, firstly because both seek the same things from the same source - they are all compradors or aspirant compradors; secondly, because the rich do not flaunt their wealth in an unbearable fashion; and, thirdly, perhaps most importantly, those who are rich are those with power - and the network of power, as described above, pervades society and prevents insurrection.

Having said all this, there is a limit to which a country like Zambia can tolerate the effects of the international recession before social divisions enforce discontent. At the same time, recession forces the elite to become more demonstrably active in the preservation of its wealth. The current situation in Zambia sees the beginning of strain, as the connecting tissue between the three parts of the urban class begins to tear.

Where does this leave the nation's intellectuals? If we take as a major case example, the university academics, we find them as members of the sub-elite. They have some elite characteristics: for instance, their learning and academic titles confer prestige upon them; but, apart from prestige, they have aglutinized very few other material values. They are not rich for one thing: a personal secretary in the Zambian private sector will earn more than a full professor. They have access and frequent intercourse with the elite: their learning means they are consulted. If they are very fortunate, they may be co-opted into the elite: every lecturer dreams of the call from State House than announces he has been, by presidential fiat, transformed into a permanent secretary, or director of a para-statal company - as sometimes happens. Academics, therefore, are members of the upper sub-elite, anxiously upwardly mobile, having the political values of the elite because their material values seem tantalisingly close. In the recession, this position means that their learning may be used to augment the power of the elite, and not used in solidarity with the poor. As the country grows poorer, the rich grow more powerful.

Challenges To Power -The Limits Of Rebellion

There have been challenges to power. Kaunda survived a coup attempt in late 1980 - an attempt, incidentally, of incredible amateurishness and ineptitude. The central conspirators had been well - placed members of the elite, anxious over the drift of the economy and seeing a remedy in even closer links with international capital and a free market at home. It might be said that they represented the right wing of a debate among the political leadership at that time, but their attempt at a coup was as incoherent as their rationale: that is, theirs was a vague feeling of discontent, coupled with a vague sense that a change of direction would improve the economy; they had no programme and no philosophy. Although they might have represented a rightist faction of UNIP, they did not actually constitute a faction. Their challenge was eccentric and individualistic.

Even so, the early 1980s were a time in which the political debate within the UNIP Central Committee seemed almost deliberately designed to provoke controversy. A move by left-wingers to brandish the term 'scientific socialism' as part and parcel of state thought drew immediate challenge from the churches. Neither side ever explained its conception of scientific socialism - except that the party conceived of inevitable progress towards prosperity once the term was accepted (a sort of vulgar declaration of historical inevitability predicated on some magic words), and the churches conceived of a Soviet-style state in which, as conventional wisdom assures us, churches are banned and Bibles are smuggled to the faithful. As it was, the active use of the term was slowly but surely withdrawn, and the churches were reassured of the Christian foundations of Humanism. But the aborted coup attempt, along with the hue and cry over 'scientific socialism', had both been devoid of intellectual content. The coup rationale was extremely generalised, and the challenge of the churches was specific to a piece of terminology which no-one understood.

In late 1980 and early 1981, the unionised copper miners went on strike for better conditions. Like the churches, the trade unions enjoy institutional freedoms: that is, they are not party wings, and they have certain, clear, constitutional rights. The copper miners form the most powerful union - since they handle the nation's single most precious commodity. They are unlike the other unions in that they constitute a labour aristocracy. They are not representative of the nation's workers, because their strategic position attracts for them special considerations and privileges. Moreover, the mines are located in a specific geographical area, and the miners have a specific tribal base which the nation's leadership cannot afford to ignore. The militancy and success of the miners is, therefore, atypical. What is typical of the Zambian labour movement is its lack of intellectual input. On this point, the mine workers and the other unions are as one. Within the mining industry, there are the beginnings of some intellectual content - but this is very much on the management side. The need for lower operating costs (the mines cost more to run than they earn; a good portion of the operating costs are local, however - while all the earnings are in foreign exchange) has brought in a flotilla of management experts, industrial psychologists, labour lawyers, and social workers, to add to the mining engineers. To date, mining personnel have been regarded as apolitical professionals. Like other professionals, doctors and lawyers, their political impact - that is, the political impact of their professions-has been very small. Whether the concentration of a new variety of educated specialists in this industry will change matters is uncertain. The mine workers union, however, seems exactly aware that, while the nation's economy pivots around the mining industry, protest can only be taken so far before the goose that lays the copper eggs is threatened. The union leadership has demonstrated a sensibility on the limits of protest that has, simultaneously, advanced the cause of these particular workers, while not seriously jeopardising the national balance of power. Those who hold political power, on the other hand, made no move to dilute the rights of unions - as they consider that these rights will not be used against their entrenched interests. An unwritten treaty limits protest and rebellion here.

Within the mine management, and the management of the public sector generally - the civil service and the extensive para-statal enterprises, not to mention the newly-established level of decentralised administration - the access to senior positions is through a narrow process of controlled patronage. Loyalists are promoted or, if incompetent, even liabilities, protected from demotion. The process of patronage tops an education system which is, itself, steadily narrowing; and which has always had, in any case, a process of narrowing built into it. The University of Zambia has only 3,000 students - out of a population of 6 million. These represent the few who survived secondary school to take high 'O' levels. Entry to secondary school is itself by examination: for the 1983/84 year, 27,000 gained entry, out of 162,000 who sat the examination. As in colonial days, primary education is the only accessible provision of learning. But, here too, increasing population, and lack of budgets for capital investment, have meant an increasing number of children out of school. The lack of classrooms and living accommodation for teachers denies educational opportunity to many - while many parents do not even seek education for their children, since they cannot afford that other colonial relic, school uniforms. To emerge from all this, and then to gain employment in the public sector, is no mean achievement. By this stage, graduates know only too well that, while Humanism forgave them their undergraduate excesses, it will not foster their career development unless they tow the party line. Intellectual protest, even intellectual commentary, rarely emanates from the public sector.

Not that channels exist for such protest and commentary. The nation's two daily newspapers are both party - controlled: that is, the party owns controlling interests;

the editors are, however, free to print what they like - but take care, again in a mood of self-censorship, to ensure that what they like is congruent with party policy. The papers do publish criticisms of the party and government, and do not escape official remonstrations, but the self-imposed band of licence in such matters is narrow. In any case, the daily circulation of the larger newspaper is only 60,000. Even if the newspapers exercise their right to genuinely free expression, or if private concerns established their own newspapers, the readership is small. The same problem bedevils publishing houses, theatres, and art galleries: there is no audience. There are, in Zambia, therefore, very few of the traditional dissidents: those associated with the arts; because there are few artists, poets, and novelists; the few who do exist retreat seriously into their art, as their circle is too small even for charlatans.

Academia Revisited: Students Like Kaunda

The University of Zambia has closed four times because of student protests. None of these closures has been as serious as some of those at the universities of Dar es Salaam and Nairobi. The closure of 1976, however, when the students protested at the government's ambiguity over the UNITA/MPLA question in Angola, led to the detention without trial of several student leaders for a year. The most recent closure, of early 1984, culminated in a dispute between the students and the Lusaka campus principal, and marked, if anything, an immature perception of internal university dialogue on both sides. The closure of 1982, however, is of some interest. Students protested the opening of a new Institute of Human Relations within the university, on the grounds that the institute was being established to give academic flesh to the scarcely-covered bones of Humanism, and used the occasion to vilify the UNIP Central Committee. The antagonism with which Humanism is greeted among student leaders (at least) is a revealing phenomenon. It is not that Humanism is without merit, but, as a social philosophy, it is considered inadequate and unscientific. If this were all, then we should have merely a debate over what constitutes social philosophy and whether ideology can be scientific. The main thrust of the student protest, however, was against the political elite who camouflaged themselves in the fine phrases of Humanism, while being, in the students' words, no better than prostitutes. They were critical of Humanism in itself, but they were more critical of its ostensible propagators. Curiously, in the midst of all this, Kaunda himself escaped strong attack.

The student leadership has, for some time now, been a national focus of resistance to UNIP - along with the mine workers. There has been no attempt, however, to establish any student-worker solidarity, or even exploratory relationships. In part, this owes to the reasonably liberal atmosphere on campus. Kaunda, as the university's Chancellor, has never delivered himself of a point-by-point defence of academic freedom. Instead, his attitude towards the students is one of paternalistic indulgence. Within limits, they may sow their wild oats; the strictures of conformity within the public service will shut them up when they enter the real world. The university is a transitional device: its graduates are transposed into the upper sub-elite, perhaps into the lower reaches of the elite; their mobility and their expectations are different from those of the miners. In larger part, however, the student diffidence towards a united anti-UNIP front owes itself to a doctrinal naivety. Although the students protest against worsening social and economic conditions, they do not initiate any social projects of their own: no neighbourhood law offices or community advice centres; not even any charity drives. They have, ironically, a similarity to the UNIP left-wing and its attraction to 'scientific socialism' and the doctrine of unabetted, automatic, historical inevitability. In short, they see no place for human agency within the historical process, and consider that material determinism will ensure true class formation and eventual rebellion - despite the pervasive UNIP presence and control in all sectors of lowest-level urban life, and despite the fact that there is no industrial structure to match the nation's urban condition, and therefore no extensive union structure - an extremely significant portion of the urban population being petty artisans, small-time entrepreneurs, short – term contract labour, thieves, black - marketeers, prostitutes, and other categories of a lumpen-proletariat. Their material condition in fact drives them into collaboration with the elite: this is seen, for instance, in the `division of labour' in the black-market, between the elite who supply the goods, and the poor who sell them.

What characterises the student position is a manifest idealism, derived second-hand from Soviet commentaries of the crudest variety, coupled with a strident insistence on their ideological correctness-based on a reading of pamphlets by Lenin and Stalin. The Marxist debates of contemporary Europe have not penetrated Zambia. Sartre's attempt at an existential Marxism is dismissed as bourgeois, because a commentary assured them that this was the case. Gramsci, Lukacs, Marcuse, Thompson, even Althusser, are only names, dismembered from any sense of Marxist debate, or of the feeling that a contemporary debate exists or is necessary. Simultaneously, Humanism is denounced for exactly the same faults of idealism, lack of scientific character, lack of rigour, lack of techniques for analysis, that the student stance is itself guilty of. In fact, this criticism of Humanism is accurate. But the student alternative merely borrows the tradition that Marxism is scientific, rigorous, etc., without actually being so.

This is a pretty sorry case, but an ironic one. For the students are probably much closer to the original Humanism of Kaunda, in terms of their ideological methodology, than the Zambian political apparatus realises. What this means is that, from within the university, no meaningful challenge of the UNIP government is likely to emerge in the foreseeable future; and no sustained, meaningful critique of it will emerge either. What should continue, however, is criticism of UNIP personalities - but this has nothing to do with intellectual development or intellectual protest.

The Institute Of Human Relations

What, then, may be expected of the controversial institute that was meant to make Humanism intellectually sustainable? The university was never enthusiastic about the institute, and is, in fact, in its current cash crisis, contemplating an intellectual retrenchment by reducing investment in all its research institutes. What we have now is a skeleton institute, which may have some skin added in due course, but which lacks any core, any heart. The institute's first director, a favourite of

Kaunda's, the British Labour peer, Lord Hatch, never gained any genuine academic recognition within the university, but did carry through a tireless publicity campaign for his institute - which the Zambian media quickly turned into a publicity campaign for himself. Zambia's only resident peer became a media star: he talks, he commentates, he is (incidentally) director of the Institute of Human Relations. His departure meant an exodus of wit and colour, but no legacy of an institute ready to roll. His successor, a Zambian social scientist, sees the institute as a seat of liberal enquiry - rather than establishing a critical base for the national philosophy.

The Next Twenty Years

In the first twenty years of independence, Zambian intellectual development has neither sustained the state in any original fashion, nor has it coherently dissented from the state. There are Zambian intellectuals, but no intellectual tradition, no discernible intellectual history. The intellectuals are supporters of the current political regimen, or fellow-travellers. Humanism, the national philosophy, remains unaltered in its public enunciation - although its boyscout purity has, thankfully, been tarnished over the years. The Zambian Left has two specific rallying points outside UNIP: the mine workers, who are in a unique position, unrelated to other social sectors, and non-intellectual; and the students, who are in transit through university, and whose political stand, while bearing all the intellectual trappings of a Marxist left, lacks any intellectual content. In no part of Zambian intellectual life does any idea contain a material force, because such ideas as there are have not been firmly grounded.

Perhaps, sometime in the next twenty years, a lone individual will arise - a great writer, perhaps: a socialist writer like Kenya's Ngugi wa Thiongo. Individualism, however, is unlikely to change society. Handled cleverly (and it was not handled cleverly in Kenya), the existence of a radical novelist or two reinforces the appearance of liberalism - particularly as his local readership is not likely to be large, so that the actual impact he has is automatically confined. As it is, there are no Zambian writers of note at present. The outstanding literary figure in residence at the university is the exiled South African, Lewis Nkosi, who rightly holds the chair in literature - but his concern is hardly located in Zambia.

What we are looking for is not individualism but an intellectual movement. There are likely to be only four intellectual centres by the year 2000. All these will be in the elite or upper sub-elite segments of society. These are: (a) the university, including both staff and students; (b) the public sector of civil service and para-statals; (c) the independent professions, but particularly the lawyers; and (d) the specialist areas of mine management. There is not likely to be any great change in the position or popularity of publishing houses; nor of the intellectualisation of the trade unions - that is, no great increase of graduates employed in their secretariats, let alone being elected to their executives. If there is to be any intellectual movement, it will emanate from one or a combination of these four groups. While each holds a critical position in society, none, by itself, commands a crucial position. Moreover, in the unlikely event of a united movement, they could be easily divided. As it is, unity in the cause of intellectual protest is remote. What may emerge is a greater amount of intellectual commentary, and this commentary, from the various intellectual centres, may converge around certain targets-though not necessarily converge firstly upon agreed formats for analysis and commentary. The outlook is for three centres of liberal commentary, and the university as a lone centre of Marxist commentary. None of this will transform society; but will at least represent an intellectual development that influences society.

As for Humanism, as mentioned at the outset of this section, this will probably not survive Kaunda. Its subsidence will engender greater intellectual activity in the political arena. For the inescapable service of Humanism has been that it filled an intellectual void in the early years of independence - when intellectual institutions were only beginning to be built, one of the hallmarks of colonialism in this region having been to refuse development to the intellect. Now, however, that institutions like the university are undergoing (a sometimes painful) adolescence, the imposition of Humanism in its unrefined state will serve only as an obstacle to a true intellectual engagement with politics; but attempts to refine Humanism are, on present evidence, unlikely to be successful.

Even within the single party structure, Humanism is an obstacle to intellectual development. For its overweening generality and do-goodiness smothers debate. It permits the development of self-interested factions in the party, but not fractions, let alone tendencies. Should, however, Zambia return to a multi-party state, then of course there will be heightened intellectual debate. Whether a return to a multi-party system is a good thing or not depends upon one's view of what constitutes democracy, and what is necessary in the historical lineage of a true single vanguard party.

An appropriate formulation would be the declaration that intellectual and ideological debate is welcomed - not in order to refine Humanism, but within the context of Humanism's general principles. By upholding Humanism as an ethic which informs philosophy and ideology, we give it its true inherent status, but limit its ambition also to be, of itself, a philosophy. Humanism's task is therefore one of requesting decency and humane qualities in the formulation and application of other, more rigorous systems of thought. Under these conditions, the future task of intellectuals and the left in Zambia is clear and unambiguous.

KAUNDA AS INTERNATIONAL CASUALTY (1987)

Dr Kenneth Kaunda, the President of Zambia, has long had a glowing press. Almost all his biographers, like Fergus MacPherson, have woven an obstinate admiration into their works, and insisted it was objectivity (32). There is no doubt that Kaunda is a great man. With the retirements of Senghor and Nyerere, he is easily the eminent statesman of Africa. His work as a nationalist who brought independence to Zambia, and his work as a champion of independence throughout southern Africa, guarantee his place in history. Kaunda is, however, a man of the mid-twentieth century – when the struggle for independence began. He was able to justify himself until 1980, when Zimbabwe became independent, and his support of armed struggle, linked with sacrifice at home was vindicated.

Is Kaunda also a man of the late-twentieth century? Is there now a palpable separation between Kaunda and his people? From the very beginning of the struggle for Zimbabwe, Kaunda and Zambia were prepared to support Zimbabwe, despite high cost, and this gained the nation, but particularly the leader, much acclaim (33). In the late-twentieth century, however, is the price of principle too high for the nation? Is this patient constituency of Kaunda now about to mutter more loudly than ever before?

The recently - established New Zealand High Commission to Zimbabwe is cross-accredited to Zambia. Before its establishment, I argued that it should be located in Zambia (34). Lusaka is the centre of diplomatic activity in southern Africa. The ANC and SWAPO are headquartered there; they and the Zambian government have long conducted an informal but increasingly public dialogue with Pretoria. What happens to Kaunda and Zambia will affect the entire region. Having said that, it is clear that Zimbabwe's international standing is rising. Its military intervention in Mozambique is a distinct, though carefully regulated, test of strength with South African regional power. Zambia, however, has refused to involve its troops in Mozambique - although, militarily, Zambian deployment alongside Zimbabwian and Tanzanian forces could be decisive in the war against the MNR.

There are two reasons for the Zambian reluctance. The first coincides with the reasoning behind Kaunda's objection to a non-aligned movement force in southern Africa, as mooted at the movement's conference in 1986. It would be a goad to South Africa beyond that country's endurance. Lusaka believes that too much is chanced, unless regulated with *precision*, in a testing of military muscle against South Africa. The second reason is that Kaunda can no longer guarantee a domestic support for Zambian international policy of this sort. The risk and expense of an expedition abroad, particularly the expense, could well spark an uprising in Zambia.

International Options

Within Lusaka, the international options are drawn up as follows. Firstly, some international policy with regard to South Africa is essential, both to continue the image of Zambia abroad as implicated in struggle, and to offset the rise of Harare and its claim to be the new capitol of southern African politics. There are, therefore, international and regional questions quite apart from what actually happens in South Africa itself.

Secondly, policy and action against South Africa must be such as to appear dynamic and purposeful, but should not alienate South Africa from continuing a diplomatic dialogue with and in Lusaka; and, particularly, should not goad South Africa into punishing Zambia in a great economic sense.

Simultaneously and thirdly, no such policy and action can be free from consequences. The most visible action, therefore, and the one that can be most regulated in undercover diplomacy with Pretoria, is the drive towards sanctions. Lusaka knows that, of all policies of international pressure, Pretoria can withstand sanctions best. In the histrionics leading to them, Lusaka hopes for a *modus vivendi* with Pretoria in the midst of them. Even so, the sanctions issue and even token South African reprisals will bite into the fragile Zambian economy. The

Zambian government must, accordingly, seek support and indulgence from the Zambian public. So far, there is no real sign this will be forthcoming.

Because of this, fourthly, Lusaka has no choice but to abstain from military adventure – because it would be more costly than economic action. This abstention needs to be presented as a virtue, allowing by default the policy of at least some sanctions.

Kaunda s Problems

Given his constraints, can Kaunda deliver this? The answer is probably either 'no' or 'with considerable difficulty.' The background to his problems are partly external - over which he has no control – and partly of his own crafting.

The orchestration of Zambian development was a music accompanied by the libretto of humanism – a social philosophy of goodness towards one's fellow man (from pre – to post feminism, goodness to one's fellow woman was never stressed). Some of the early prognoses about goodness bringing forth material rewards were unbelievably gushing (35). The role and ability of (at best) an abstraction, or (at worst) a sermon, could never fill hungry bellies. At all times, the libretto has overcome music. There are many words about development, but little development (36).

One of the features of Zambian politics that prevent development is the inescapable tendency towards centralisation. There have been attempts at decentralisation, but they have not been successful (37). The fact is that, in a one-party state, political centralisation finds it difficult to cope with and allow administrative and developmental decentralisation. The demand for political control has meant, firstly, that the Party acts as a great commissar: no aspect of government is possible without the Party's political direction. Secondly, it means that Party service must be rewarded. Since, even in a one-party state, party sinecures are limited, the Party must use its control over the government to appoint party members to an increasing number and range of government positions. The Party triumphs over the technocracy. While development suffers, those whose position actively obstructs or slows down development enjoy the rewards of appointed office; live somewhat better than the average citizen; drive white cars.

Sophisticated Operation

None of this should present a caricaturised view of the one-party state in Zambia. It is a sophisticated operation. There are dissenting members of parliament, even though of the official Party. There are a greater range of civil liberties, with a record of enforceability, than almost anywhere in Africa (38). And, under certain conditions, the biographies of those who opposed Kaunda may be written and published (39). There is an active trade union movement on the Zambian Copperbelt, centred on the miners; these workers have not, however, had much influence in the south of the country, and have found no alliance with the educated professions, or with the students.

As will be noted later, however, all three groups share a common critique of Zambian society. In the meantime, the Party forms an identifiable object in Zambian politics and development. It forms Kaunda's base; but it is a base in which political control has been seen to represent a channelling of economic reward, and an obstruction or at least incompetence in arranging the economic reward of the nation at large. There is a tension in Kaunda's base.

External Limits

As with almost all African countries, the IMF has become the lender of first resort. This is because commercial credit is no longer willing to loan to Africa. It is also because the economic problems of Africa now require a planned and co-ordinated liquidity. The IMF provides liquidity, but its sense of planning and co-ordination are unattractive in the extreme to African populations. The conditionality of IMF loans hits hardest at those least able to bear the blows. A central plank in the IMF platform is the reduction of public expenditure. In Zambia, this meant the lifting of subsidies on the staple food, resulting in almost a 100 per cent price rise just before Christmas 1986. The result was nationwide riots. After some days of this, Kaunda relented and the prices came down again; but he had been humiliated, and protest had been seen to succeed.

The other IMF imposition on Zambia has been the establishment of an auctioning system for foreign exchange. Such systems have operated in the past in Sudan and Uganda, and are now also in place in Nigeria and Ghana. Very briefly, the concept behind them is to make foreign exchange available in such a way as to meet true demand. If people truly want and need foreign exchange, they will pay for it. Secondly, the system is intended to reduce or obliterate recourse to the black market for foreign exchange – since, effectively, open bidding under official supervision should realise the 'market rate' that would otherwise have been offered by the black market. The system, therefore, satisfies true demand and, simultaneously, restores monetary control to the government.

Obvious Flaws

There are obvious flaws to this sort of thinking. Firstly, true demand is not necessarily measured by the amount of local currency one has to bid for foreign exchange. Key industries and agricultural sectors can no longer afford foreign exchange and do not bid, though their contribution to development is vital. In this sense, development can be marginalised in the name of fiscal regulation. Secondly, in an import-dominated economy, as Zambia's is, the price of imports must rise. The price of purchasing foreign exchange must be passed on to the consumer of the goods bought and imported with that foreign exchange. Inflation rises as a result; but there is no offsetting increase in export receipts. (The Zambian copper mines made a 56 million kwacha loss in 1985-86).

Thirdly, it means that there is no set exchange rate for the national currency, so future economic planning becomes notional. (Zambia is worse off here than other examples, having no official or government tier at which an exchange rate is fixed for official transactions, leaving the private sector to bid at tiers above it). Despite all these deficiencies, when the Zambian government felt moved to intervene in the auction, to stabilise the kwacha at 9-12 to the dollar in early 1987, the IMF was furious. Nevertheless, there are clear limits to the number of transgressions against IMF conditionality that Kaunda can take. Because of this, he is increasingly being portrayed as the IMF's hireling, and the Zambian people as a hostage to (what seems to be fictional) fortune.

Certain Movements

All this has meant much shuffling in the corridors of power in Lusaka. On 14 January 1987, Kaunda sacked the army commander, General Christon Tembo. This may have been due to nervousness rather than real evidence of a coup in plot. Nevertheless, the new senior command of the armed forces are all Kaunda loyalists. There is, however, much speculation surrounding the intentions of Grey Zulu, a long-time Kaunda loyalist, and the Party Secretary-General. He has made some very muted criticisms of Kaunda. If this swings Party support away from Kaunda and towards Zulu, an interesting situation could develop.

Zulu is not a technocrat. He is heavily identified with the Party, and all its past mistakes. He has always used, however, a peculiar left-wing terminology, and this has made him an occasional darling of the students and the Zambian intelligentsia. It is possible that he, as a non-technocrat, could bring technocrats in his tow. They would only have a place, however, if other Party appointees were made to move over, and Zulu would have too many debts to pay after any competition with Kaunda to be able to do that.

No Solution

Moreover, a Zulu ascendancy solves nothing for the students in the long run. They have consistently championed a *dependentista* analysis of Zambian society, where an economic and political elite acts as a *comprador* or collaborationist class, satisfying its avariciousness by complicity with foreign plunderers – in this case, the capitalist states and corporations, and the international capitalist system that incorporates (or depends upon) the IMF.

This view if the world, in its more vulgar representations, is shared by many segments of society at large – including the miners. Though a labour aristocracy in a land with new formal sector jobs, they have also seen their earning power suffer and their cost of living rise. Simultaneously, the mine management pampers itself with expensive new office blocks (marble-clad) and executive aircraft; and still includes in its number a highly visible contingent of white expatriates. Those members of the professional classes who, meanwhile, find that entry into the elite is now harder than it was might yet remember their student beliefs; and, thus, bring into being a curious tripartite alternative to the Party. It would, however, probably be too unwieldy ever to succeed.

Sustained Critique

There has been, for many years, a sustained critique of Zambian foreign policy on the grounds that it serves the *comprador* class (40). How this critique has been sustained in the face of Kaunda's principles and their high price to date has always astounded me. There is no doubt, however, that the drive within Zambia is to mute the foreign policy of Kaunda. The drive is against sanctions and militarism on the grounds of domestic cost. At the same time, this conservative desire is linked to a radical one, which is also a naively hopeful one – and that is to resist IMF conditionality. In short, there is an all-spectrum insistence upon domestic comfort or, at least, limits to domestic discomfort.

There is really no way this twin-horned insistence can be met by any government – under Kaunda, Zulu, or a technocrat-labour alliance. What can be done is to mollify the effects of one by capitulation in the other. This is, to harbour as many funds as possible in the face of IMF conditionality by suspending all foreign policy initiatives and their high priced principles. In short, it would mean a withdrawal of Zambia from southern African action and calculation, a diminution of Zambian power and influence in the Organisation of African Unity, the non-aligned movement, and the United Nations. It would mean, tartly, the end to nobility in the region – a nobility which has always been personified by Kaunda and championed by him (41).

Is the true question, therefore, one of whether in the late-twentieth century, there is any longer, room for nobility in southern Africa? This may well be the case. For the West, there is a need to have Zambia as a stable nation in a turbulent region. A Zambia that withdraws its foreign policy will suit the West, no matter how introspective it becomes. The West has always admired, but never supported, Kaunda and Zambia. In New Zealand, as we learnt finally of our need to recognise Africa, we also looked beyond Zambia, and looked at the glamour of independence by armed struggle in Zimbabwe, and the romance of a future Zimbabwe in armed conflict with South Africa. It is a fine voyeurism. Not having helped the pioneer actor, will we help the successor?

Addendum

Since this section was written, President Kaunda has taken a number of decisive economic measures. They include a repudiation of the IMF economic programme for Zambia; the abolition of the foreign currency auction and the consequent fixing of an exchange rate for the Kwacha; the imposition of further import controls; the cutting of interest rates; and the limiting of interest repayments on foreign debt to five per cent of foreign exchange earnings.

These were exceptionally courageous steps to take and they have restored some of Kaunda's domestic popularity and presidential stability. Having said that, there are still danger signs. Firstly, the increase in import controls must be viewed against the fact that Zambia in 1986 imported only 25 per cent of what it imported a decade earlier. There is a limit to how many sacrifices can be made by a population and infrastructure heavily dependent on imports. Secondly, repudiation of the IMF programme must mean extreme caution on the part of other leaders in debt rescheduling or fresh loans; liquidity could become a problem here. Thirdly, the self-limitation of interest repayments may not long be politically sustainable. It is a defiance of orthodox fiscal behaviour and expectation. In short, the international screws will come on at this point in particular. All this means that Kaunda has bought himself and his country some time. In the long and even medium term, however, the situation remains a desperate one.

Finally, there are rumours that a Zambian military contingent is deployed in Mozambique. This is not officially acknowledged and, in line with the reasoning of the article, I do not think it can be acknowledged or unofficially reinforced beyond a token military presence.

KAUNDA AND SOUTHERN AFRICA: IMAGE AND REALITY IN FOREIGN POLICY (1989)

This section introduces a wider study to be entitled, *Kaunda in Southern Africa: Towards an Intellectual History of Foreign Policy* (42). Literature on Zambia and Kaunda, and on southern Africa generally, has considered Zambian foreign policy firstly from the agreed premise that the president plays the major and decisive role in policy formulation, and secondly from two opposed views of him. A distinction exists between Kaunda as a noble statesman and as a collaborator with the forces of oppression. No study has been made to assess the merits of two competing schools.

The wider the study intends to investigate Kaunda's foreign policy both before and after Zimbabwe's liberation and independence. Before independence, a free Zimbabwe was the principle plank of Kaunda's foreign policy platform. After independence, Zimbabwe competed for and successfully gathered what had been Zambia's crown of regional leadership against South Africa. Simultaneously, Zambia's economic position began seriously to worsen. These two unconnected events were traumatic to Zambian self-confidence and policy. The wider study has, therefore, two levels of comparison: comparison between two images of Kaunda, each promoted by a separate school; and comparison of Kaunda's foreign policy in two time periods – before and after 1980.

In addition, the wider study hopes to make use of theoretical materials in conflict analysis and mediation; and also from the field of strategic studies. These forms of comparison and these theoretical approaches give the study a sub-title, 'Towards an Intellectual History of Foreign Policy', and such an approach has not been attempted before. The aim of the present paper is to introduce some of these considerations and, in particular, to discuss in outline form the history of Kaunda's mediation in southern African affairs, suggesting the problems that arise in any such discussion.

A full discussion of these problems, however, would probably see them listed as follows:

1. There is a contradiction in Kaunda's method. Zambia is a party to the dispute in southern Africa and Kaunda should, therefore, be concerned with endogenous dispute management. However, he consistently behaves as if he were an outside third party, using exogenous methods.

2. Related to this is the question of the extent of Kaunda's objectivity, as opposed to his bias, or his quest for subjective goals. Does he search for a peace in the region which accommodates all parties, including the South African Government, or is he scoring national points?

3. The questions of method and goals raise one of procedure. He engages in bilateral diplomacy (at summit and other meetings) with South Africa, but has no multilateral agenda authorised by frontline states.

4. In his bilateral diplomacy there is a question of power and substance. What is there, by himself, that Kaunda can offer that balances or neutralises the coercive diplomacy that South Africa uses?

5. Is the relationship between Kaunda and South Africa one in which a pole of legitimacy stands contrasted to a pole of power? Is this a deliberate contrast, in which Kaunda's oft-paraded moralism plays a major part?

These questions of endogenous vs exogenous method, of levels of disinterestedness, of bilateralism vs multilaterialism, of coercive diplomacy and power of vs legitimacy take their place within the already established questions of the academic literature.

1. Does Kaunda (who personifies, depending on the source, a class or a nation) act in a manner which is complicit with or opposed to South African hegemony in the region?

2. In the terms established by the *dependentista* school, is he a *comprador*?

3. In the more general terms of the early literature on Kaunda, is his foreign policy one of nobility or debased nobility?

Two Schools of Thought

Of the frontline states, Tanzania (1961) and Zambia (1964) are the oldest. Zambia however has been the more directly involved in confronting South African policy and white racism. UDI in Rhodesia in 1965 meant that the newly-independent Zambia was almost immediately plunged into a situation with high regional and foreign policy stakes. If Zambia has been long a direct participant in southern African affairs, its president Kenneth Kaunda, has long been an enigma to those who would wish to see a consistent and logically-framed Zambian foreign policy. For the South Africans, understanding Kaunda has been a long-term exercise in which admiration has been rotated with bemusement. There have been, however, sufficient serious engagements between Kaunda and South African leaders to suggest that he is regarded by them as a regional actor with a fine appreciation of *realpolitik* under his crafted rhetoric and occasional flights of fancy. He is, in short, approachable in political terms: conscious of the need to exchange items of value, and mindful of limits and how they might be negotiated, imposed and enforced. It is this form of political intercourse with South Africa that has led a school of critics to describe Kaunda and the (as yet, ill-defined) grouping of well-off Zambians as a *comparador* class.

In the field of southern African studies, the *dependentista* thesis has been most asserted by the Canadian scholar, Timothy Shaw. Zambia was an early and repeated target for Shaw's critique, perhaps because some of his early academic career was spent there (43). Since that time, the volume of his work, based on this approach has been staggering (44).

Following in his footsteps have been a number of other writers. With them, as with Shaw, Zambia has been a common case-study. (45) I have several times elsewhere questioned some of the premises and analyses of this school. (46) At this point, however, the *dependentista* approach should be seen in contra-distinction to Kaunda's earlier, extremely favourable press.

The early reputation stemmed in large part from the idealism of Kaunda's writing. With Dominic Mulaisho, Kaunda represents Zambian literature in then pioneering Heinemann list (47). No international publisher has issued works by any other Zambian author. There are a variety of reasons, including monetary ones, for this; but what it means is that, in the intellectual and literary worlds, Kaunda tended to dominate through lack of competition. This sense of loneness and centredness is apparent also in foreign policy formulation, and I wish to return to this below. The literary perception of Kaunda as idealist, as principled moralist, was reinforced by a succession of his books, all offering variations of a humanist theme, with 'humanism' being a vague compound of Christian and socialist thought peculiar to Kaunda, but elevated by him and his party to the status of national social philosophy. (48) The effect of these books permeated assessments of his foreign policy. His approach to the UDI of Rhodesia was described as costly but proper, as the "high price of principle". (49) It is not that principle was lacking; it was there in measurable abundance; but such treatments of Kaunda's foreign policy misplaced or overlooked the full measure of its opportunism, deceit and mistakes. Finally, as Kaunda's literary discussions on humanism were elevated nationally, reaction in the west was enthusiastic and endorsing. Kaunda secured an influential group of British church-based supporters. European writers and academics produced gushing treatises on humanism (50). A succession of biographers made him into almost a black philosopher-king (51). Even the People's Republic of China sought to orchestrate his endorsement of Mao's vaguely philosophic 'Three World Theory' (52). Only in the 1980s has there been any sign of disenchantment within this club of support. (53)

Between these two schools of thought, is there a way forward? There are some worthwhile points to make about Kaunda. Within the context of a one-party state, the Zambian record on human rights has been fair. (54) I have noted elsewhere that the freeness of elections (again in the one-party context) has been observable. (55) Notwithstanding the lip-service paid to humanism and its shallowness as a social philosophy, it has some value as a normative ethic (56). Kaunda's accomplishment in keeping united a nation of more than seventy tribal groups, some like the Lozi with a history of determined independence, has been impressive. Finally, despite the ambiguity surrounding many of Kaunda's efforts at mediation in southern Africa, it cannot be denied he is in some way committed to the concept of mediation. He has sought to mediate in conflicts outside southern Africa, such as those in Chad and the Western Sahara, where no charges of wheeling and dealing with racist and imperial capital could be levelled against him. Having said that, there are two other points to make. The first is that poverty in Zambia has very greatly increased in the last five years. The incoherence of Kaunda's economic policy has rightly led to his being viewed internationally as someone approaching the end of his intellectual tether. (57) Secondly, any examination of Zambian public administration would isolate Kaunda as, himself, the foreign policy establishment, machinery, lone formulator. It is certainly right to focus on him.

A Note on Public Administration and Policy Formation

The Zambian foreign policy apparatus appears to have distinct levels where policy formulation can occur. These are the Ministry of Foreign Affairs (professional level), the Cabinet Ministers of Foreign Affairs and Defence (political level), the United National Independence Party's Central Committee (akin to a politburo, and not just a supreme party level but the nation's formal policy formulation level), and the President with his advisers in State House (executive level). Much the same structure applies to all areas of domestic policy. Having said that, it should be pointed out that the Zambian elite has a remarkably informal nature. There can be much movement among these levels and consultations can make artificial any study of Zambian political society that binds these levels to their face value. Foreign policy formulation, however, is an exception.

These are official levels. There are no effective unofficial ones. The unofficial side to a foreign policy 'establishment' does not exist. No Zambian has issued a formal study of his nation's foreign policy; there is no institute of international affairs; the newspapers are critical of government domestic policy within limits, but do not seriously comment on foreign policy; the university's involvement with international relations as a discipline is a recent and low-key one.

Within the official levels, the absence of unofficial ones has had an impact. The lack of academic training has meant that research inputs for all official levels can be very rudimentary indeed. Decisions can be made often on intuition rather than assessed data. Entry and promotion within the professional level is not dependent on academic qualifications. As it has become harder to gain entry to civil service positions because of the increasing need for economic and other social scientific skills, the Ministry of Foreign Affairs has been accused as a last bastion for patronage - where the lack of qualifications can cause no immediately measurable harm. As it is, the Ministry formally represents Zambia's position abroad; it represents policy, and it is not its formulator. To a large extent, this is true even of ministers at the political level. Their access to policy formers and to the president himself can be wide or limited, depending on the minister concerned; but rotation of ministers, a common Zambian practice, means little time to master a portfolio whose most public expression is accompaniment of the president on his own foreign excursions, or at his announcement of policy he has decided upon, after having conceived his own options in the first place. There have been a number of studies of public administration in Zambia; (58) none, however, has considered the roles of ministry and minister in foreign affairs and their marginal involvement in policy formulation. No published study has been made, furthermore, on the role of the Central Committee in Zambian policy formation-precisely because its existence as a policy body is contentious. The IMF has been known to question the desirability of two tiers of administration, political and party, with parallel and expensive functions in a poor society. For the party to act as a gigantic commissar to the Zambian political machine, it too requires a proper research input. Here, as at the political level, research into foreign policy is rudimentary. The Central Committee, moreover, has increasingly become a higher cabinet of time-servers and erstwhile trouble-makers who have been co-opted to the highest level possible, because the president can most easily control them there. Its originality and sense of insight have not gained high reputations.

This leaves State House and the President, where a fully executive approach to foreign policy is found. It has not always been so. Zambia's first Foreign Minster, Vernon Mwaanga, was widely regarded as a major figure with considerable influence on policy (59). Other identifiable names in the policy formulation process have included Mark Chona, whose version of shuttle diplomacy in the middle 1970s was as striking in the regional context as Kissinger's was at large. Chona's exploits were never sung, as Kissinger's were. He was, besides, a member of Kaunda's State House staff, and this leaves only Mwaanga as a lone representation of influence on policy outside it. With both Mwaanga and Chona's retirements from public life, no similar figure has emerged. In recent history, certainly from the independence of Zimbabwe onwards, Kaunda has dominated foreign policy formulation.

Foreign Policy up to the Independence of Zimbabwe

Within a very short time of UDI in Rhodesia, commentators were speaking of Kaunda's principles and the cost to Zambia of confronting an illegal regime on its southern borders. Certainly it seemed a harsh circumstance, with Zambian independence having been achieved only in 1964 and the Rhodesian UDI being declared in November 1965. Moreover, as the 1960s drew to a close, and copper prices began to decline on international markets, it seemed that Zambia was undergoing a siege of sorts. There were certainly harsh adjustments that had suddenly been made. The Zambians had always complained that, during the days of Confederation, mineral wealth from the Zambian north had been directed to the development of the Rhodesian south. There has been both some truth and a degree of envy in this complaint; but it meant that, after UDI, the Zambians had to deploy new and expensive infrastructures. The Maamba mine in Zambia's Southern Province was geared up to replace Rhodesia's Wankie as the main source of coal and coke. But it was not until 1973 that a really major crisis can be said to have occurred between Zambia and Rhodesia, one that threatened Zambia's entire economic viability. This crisis involved the misreading of signals by both Smith and Kaunda, a dramatic and unprepared decision by Kaunda to stand on a combination of pride and sudden principle, and an attempt by South Africa to preserve Zambian interests. This was the first of three major incidents throughout the 1970s in which South African and Zambian interests converged, and bespoke a South African view of Zambia's value in the region. Until 1973, however, although Zambia had been forced to make large expenditures in a shortened time frame, there had been a degree of bluff and purposely plaintiff pleading in Zambia's expression of its position. In the west, Kaunda's constituency of supporters carried the banner of wounded hero for him.

In 1973, however, after a border incident, Smith suddenly closed the Zambian/Rhodesian border. This was meant to generate publicity for the Rhodesian account of the incident, and to act as a large though clumsy warning to Zambia against the repetition of border 'provocations'. Ten hours later, Smith proposed to exempt copper from this closure; and, three weeks later, he proposed to lift the closure entirely. Smith had come under some pressure from Pretoria to rescind his border closure. To his surprise, however, he found Kaunda adamant in refusing to accept the re-opened border. Smith, said Kaunda, was 'too hostile a neighbour', and could not be trusted - though, in the matter of cross-border traffic, Kaunda had trusted Smith for almost eight years.

Kaunda's decision suddenly to boycott the rail routes south meant a scramble for alternatives. None of the scramble had been prepared beforehand, and it brought great economic hardship. The copper exports, upon which Zambia's economic viability rested, had to be rerouted northwards, much of it on the Benguela railway through Angola. The only problem here was that, having refused to treat with one minority government, Zambia had now to treat with the Portuguese variety in Angola. The task, however, of shifting 27,000 tons of copper a month was daunting; and, by the end of 1974, British newspapers were full of exposes of how, against proclaimed principles, Zambia had been secretly using Rhodesian railways to move copper to Mozambican ports (60). Principle, however, cannot conjure lifelines to the sea overnight - although it must be said (and even with hindsight the effort seems miraculous) that the frantic building of the Tazara railway, linking Zambia with the Tanzanian port of Dar es Salaam, built with Chinese aid and cooperation after western powers refused to help, was an extraordinary achievement. The Chinese propaganda films about it, depicting Chinese and Zambian labourers side by side, startled habituated viewers; in the same way that Zhou Enlai's send off speech to the Chinese volunteers stirred a genuine romance with Africa. He predicted that many of the volunteers would die from the work and conditions in Africa, and many of them did. Their commitment startled their Zambian counterparts, and the ferocity of the Chinese input to the railway remains a Zambian legend. Tazara was opened in October 1975, and, after two years of uncertainty, Zambia had an assured and uncompromised access to the sea. It was hardly a moment too soon, as the Benguela railway ceased to operate in the midst of the Angola civil war.

At talks between the South African Prime Minister Vorster and Kaunda in 1975, Vorster offered to vouch safe the reopening of the Zambian/Rhodesian frontier. Kaunda refused to agree to this. Perhaps he had in mind the viability of Tazara. Three years later, in October 1978, rail links with Rhodesia were restored - the agreement to do so being signed by rail authorities rather than by government leaders-and Zambia began exporting copper and fertilizer for shipping from Port Elizabeth in South Africa. The 1975 meeting between Vorster and Kaunda was, however, an extraordinary affair, in which the question of rail links was set against the broader framework of a regional *detente* which could be accomplished and epitomised by summit meetings of engaging candour. At the 1975 meeting, Vorster asked Kaunda why he could not agree to a re-opened border. Tucked away in a footnote, Deon Geldenhuys gives Vorster's recollection of Kaunda's answer: “Julius won't let me do it." (61) The moves for a regional detente had divided the southern African states. Kaunda felt himself being lulled by the prospect of a conflict-free region on the one hand, and lectured on principle by Nyerere on the other. The long standing tension between the two leaders has never been properly studied.

The broad framework of the 1975 meeting, however, concerned the shape of the region after Portugal's withdrawal from it. Rail links, transition to some form of a majority rule in Rhodesia, and the shape of political intercourse between the southern African states and South Africa comprised the agenda. In the brief period between the Portuguese decision to withdraw and the collapse of the Alvor Agreement, leading to the MPLA ascendancy in Angola, it seemed as if South Africa wished to come to terms with a region in which the balance of power had been changed. With the input of substantially increased Soviet aid and Cuban troops in Angola, the South Africans felt that the balance of power was in danger of changing too far, and themselves launched a military intervention, bringing to a close all talks about a *detente*. Kaunda's lingering hope that UNITA might find a place in the government of Angola, a hope he still held at the beginning of 1976, led to student riots and the first closing of the University of Zambia. For the students of that year, the demonstrations in favour of the MPLA and the struggles against police closure of the campus, followed by the imprisonment of several student leaders, were a coming of age. It is 1976 rather than 1968 that is part of the student legend there. At the same time as Kaunda faced pressure from the left in the form of university students, he faced contrary pressure from the right, as businessmen rallied conservative political support for the re-opening of the Rhodesian border. Kaunda would have liked to have done just that; but felt he could only move to do so within a new regional arrangement that ensured majority rule in Rhodesia. For the South Africans, a black-ruled Rhodesia was a possibility, but only within a region they felt safe in. The high communist profile in Angola rendered the region unsafe in South African eyes. Kaunda's residual hopes for UNITA, coupled with his denunciation by the students, who also began to criticise the 'non-scientific' and bourgeois nature of Zambian humanism, provided a key entry point for the *dependentista* school to label him a *comprador*. (62)

Even writers sympathetic to Kaunda judge that he talked too long to the South Africans, past any point when negotiations could have been useful or made any difference. (63) Why then had Kaunda kept talking? And why did the South Africans want particularly to talk to him in the first place? Looking at the period 1973-9, the South Africans had taken an interest in the Zambian position three times:

1) In 1973, when Smith closed the border, the South Africans insisted that he open it again. They sought then an economically and politically viable Zambia that they could talk to. That Kaunda refused to accept the re-opening of the border must have seemed both petulant and bizarre to the South Africans.

2) In 1975, after the Portuguese decision to withdraw from southern Africa, the South Africans talked to Kaunda about a new political basis for the region. Botswana's Kharma took an interest in the talks and encouraged the idea of *detente*, but it was Kaunda who was a principal at the talks, not him.

3) Throughout the Anglo-American initiative, and at key points throughout the Commonwealth and British initiative for majority-rule in Rhodesia, spanning the period 1977-9, high-level contact was maintained between the Zambian and South African capitals, as each set of leaders looked over its shoulder at the other, and while each sought to take the initiative, each was mindful of not outpacing the other.

Already in Vorster's time, and in a more refined sense in Botha's, the South Africans saw Zambia as a key actor in *their region*. As such, Zambia was a prize of a specific nature. The size and wealth of Zambia, relative to the other southern African states, and the distinguished international reputation of the Zambian President, would have lent credibility to any regional concord in which both Zambia and South Africa were involved – far more so, for instance, than any concord with, say, Malawi; or a customs union with the region's weak states. Botha's early sense of a constellation in which Zambia would be the last and politically most valuable asset was a development of this basic view. For his part, Kaunda would have known of his usefulness in the South African outlook, but sought to exploit it for his own sense of possibility. Perhaps the region could move, even if slowly towards liberation by peaceful and judiciously balanced means. To win liberation meant costs and dangers. Part of these costs and dangers were to his own nation. Both within his nation and the region, the costs were measured in terms that affronted his humanism. The curious mixture of genuine principle and genuine opportunism, mixed further with petulance and a degree of plain wishfulness, have made him enigmatic even to the Zambian political community.

In any case, and here Kaunda's supporters have firm ground, he is not against liberation by war. He is for liberation without war if it can possibly, perhaps even remotely be achieved. From 1977, Zambia harboured ZAPU personnel and ZIPRA military bases for Nkomo. In May 1977, Smith delivered a warning to Kaunda on the dangers of this: and from 1978 to 1979, through the Lancaster House talks, right up to the arrival of Lord Soames as Governor in Salisbury, Rhodesia openly raided Zambia, launching several commando attacks and two major air raids. Roads and bridges were destroyed; Nkomo's residence in Lusaka was destroyed; other ZAPU houses in Lusaka were attacked. Zambia responded by air-raid blackouts and, at one point, a military mobilisation of the urban male population. But the Zambian military were placed under strict orders not to counter-attack, or even to fire a shot in self-defence without clearance from State House itself. No such authorisation ever came. It was a support for war and an endurance of war that was doggedly pacific. Kaunda's admirers said it demonstrated his commitment to principle. His detractors said it was because he feared Zambian involvement in hostilities would escalate them and possibly lead to a direct South African involvement. The essential point here is that, having accepted the failure of *detente* in 1976, Zambia was ready to support Nkomo's military endeavours from 1977. Kaunda never abandoned his interest and involvement in negotiations; hence his deep commitment to the Commonwealth efforts in 1979 and to the Lancaster House talks that followed. But, alongside this, even if within a somewhat ambivalent context, Zambia made its commitment to military struggle for a new Zimbabwe.

Foreign Policy after the Independence of Zimbabwe

The independence of Zimbabwe compounded Zambia's foreign policy problems. The emergence of an economically-stronger state that attracted an immense international goodwill meant that Zambia's regional and international positions were diminished. Regionally, the economic pole passed from Zambia to Zimbabwe: the possibility of an alternative or, at least, partial relief from economic dependency on Pretoria was now offered by Harare. Lusaka had never been able to provide this sort of centre for the majority-ruled southern African states, but both the concept and real possibility of one was appropriated overnight by the new Zimbabwean state. Internationally, Kaunda's method of attracting influential sympathisers through his sense of nobility and his nation's suffering seemed to have lost momentum. The international media lost no time in building up Mugabe as the new black prince, reflecting the official views of western governments as they did so. Besides, had not Kaunda's principles been directed towards a free Zimbabwe? Now that a free state had emerged, the Zambian enterprise seemed historical. In 1980, a mass downgrading of diplomatic missions in Lusaka took place, with new missions being established in Harare. If Kaunda could no longer parade Lusaka as a diplomatic capital for the region, his appearance as a mobiliser of international opinion on southern Africa would no longer look convincing.

Kaunda has more specific problems with the new state; for it was a state ruled by a ZANU Government. Kaunda had supported the ZAPU party of Nkomo. On the surface, much tribute was laid at the feet of Zambia's involvement in the liberation war. The reality of relationship between the two states can be appreciated by the fact that Kaunda felt able to make his first state visit to Zimbabwe only in July 1981, more than a year after independence, and only after Machel and Nyerere had made their own state visits and been accorded the accolades of sponsors of liberation. Despite his belated state visit, the return to the bush of Ndebele dissidents, leading to unrest in the Matabelelands, did nothing to dispel Zimbabwean suspicions of Kaunda. Was he still supporting Nkomo?

Kaunda certainly tried to assert Lusaka's primacy in the majority - ruled region. The formal foundation of SADCC took place under the Lusaka Declaration of its principles. Zimbabwe was invited to join even before its independence celebrations, and the impression sought was one of a new and young state acceding to a regional movement initiated by older and wiser figures who were kindly solicitous of the youngster. This, of course, flew in the face of Zimbabwe's greater wealth and infra-structure, and its natural position as economic pole, but the Zambian effort was made nonetheless. In international circles, Zambia tried its best to encourage and put pressure upon the western Contact Group of five nations concerned with independence for Namibia (64). As the 1980s decade progressed, Zambia sought also a primary position in Chester Crocker's regular round of consultations in southern Africa. And, in 1988, on the eve of the peace-talks between Angola and South Africa, Zambia actively sought a role as mediator between the two parties (as had Egypt and Nigeria), mindful of the kudos any even partially successful mediation would bring. Zambia was also mindful that, unlike other countries seeking a mediatory role, it had long conducted a dialogue with South Africa. This dialogue had continued after Zimbabwe's independence, had bemused and outraged other frontline presidents, and had included a major face-to-face conference between Kaunda and Botha.

This summit took place in Botswana at Kaunda's request (the Botswana President stressing that he was providing space for the meeting upon request, and then politely but studiously distancing himself from the entire episode). There appeared no particular reason for the summit. The time at which it was held, April 1982, was not auspicious in any sense, and Zambia had not itself been attacked by South African forces, apart from one border incident at Shesheke, near the Caprivi Strip, in September 1981. By April 1982, however, the South African ‘total strategy' of economic and military destabilization was being fully implemented. Perhaps Kaunda wished to discuss that, although it seems that the meeting never rose above generalities. In any case, the full implications of total strategy were appreciated only with hindsight - the trail of devastation having first to be laid before it could be linked to any master plan. In early 1982, the trail of devastation, although embarked upon, had still far to go. This is not to say that the devastation had been trivial.

South African forces, in their Operation Protea, had penetrated deeply into Angola. Afterwards in 1984 and with the signing of the Lusaka Accord between Angola and South Africa, signalling the *Pax Pretoriana*, Kaunda was to claim that his mediation efforts, beginning from the 1982 summit, had been successful. The *Pax Pretoriana*, however, probably emerged from South African satisfaction with the results of total strategy by then, with non-aggression pacts signed between South Africa on the one side and Swaziland and Mozambique on the other; the Lusaka Accord being, though not an equivalent to Nkomati, somewhere along the line towards it. Pretoria had high hopes of Nkomati-style accords with Angola and other southern African states. For Kaunda to claim mediatory success in 1984, at a stage of initial South African satisfaction with total strategy, particularly when, at the 1982 summit, Kaunda could not have appreciated the value and nature of total strategy and what it would seek to achieve in the next two years, was either gullibility on his own party or a search for a gullible audience.

An even more bizarre attempt at mediation in May 1984, when Kaunda hosted in Lusaka representatives of SWAPO *and* the internal Namibian parties, *together with* the South African Administrator-General for South West Africa. At this conference on the future of Namibia and progress towards independence, Kaunda occupied the chair at one point for a marathon 20 hours, seeking to impose all his moral authority upon the splintered Namibians. The South African Administrator-General, who had helped keep them splintered in the first place, alternated with Kaunda as chairman.

It would seem that Kaunda never abandoned his hope for a regional *detente* with South Africa. With the signatures of the Lusaka and Nkomati Accords, and the revelation of the Swaziland accord, all taking place or being made known in early 1984, the notion of a *Pax Pretoriana* was widely broadcast. It seemed that certain concessions might be wrung from Pretoria. But, even if peace in the region was possible, it was a peace very much on Pretoria's terms. It was a peace in name; in reality it was a respite from South African violence. It was a dictated peace, and one offered after a pattern of South African regional policy had been implemented and reached its initial objectives. Violence had been used to secure accords which recognised, in one degree or another, South Africa's military strength and capabilities in the region. An agreement to withdraw from Angola (which took a year to implement and which, in any case, left UNITA in place), and an agreement to withdraw support from RENAMO in Mozambique (never honoured), represented a level of commitment significantly below that of an agreement to withdraw from Namibia. Appearing to give up strategic advances is one thing, particularly if they can be reclaimed. Giving up a strategic base is another. For Kaunda to launch an initiative of this nature, within a South African peace, seemed naive.

A Concept of Two Poles

This type of behaviour either leaves Kaunda open to charges of naivety or of collaborationism. If not an economically and class-based *compradorism*, it can resemble a political collaboration with Pretoria. To a certain extent, it is. A country doesn't have to sign an accord with South Africa to realise that it dominates the region. A relationship with South Africa is inevitable and must inevitably recognise its military and economic power. To challenge South Africa on its own terms is impossible. Yet, to allow South Africa's regional hegemony to go unchallenged would be unbearable. The attempt, therefore, must be to find new terms for a challenge. There must be a sustainable and credible challenge, otherwise there is no mutually-observed *detente* - merely an imposed peace. Kaunda wanted the mutual recognition of different strengths in the region. If South Africa recognised certain strengths in Zambia, it might not easily apply its own strengths against Kaunda's state, and the majority-ruled region might have some sort of not fully-trammelled rallying point.

Notwithstanding genuine if residual principle and idealism in Kaunda's foreign policy, Kaunda had deliberately *used* his moral image in the region's diplomacy. It has been, at times, an opportunistic, even cynical, usage. It has become soiled and has lain Kaunda open to criticism. Kaunda had a blinding flash of principle in 1973, and this proved very costly. Since 1975, principle has been something deliberately tailored and used as a diplomatic and negotiating instrument, and not as something pure in its own sense. It is *portrayed* internationally as pure, but that is part of a foreign policy to gain as many influential friends as possible. South Africa has sought a region dominated by its power; Kaunda has sought a region in which *the pole of power is confronted by a pole of legitimacy*. To use this term is to do two things. Firstly, it seeks to encapsulate a view of Kaunda's foreign policy. It may not be a correct view, but I think it is one worth further exploration. Secondly, it predisposes exploration of the issue along certain lines. The concept of a pole of power versus a pole of legitimacy is one which exists in the mainstream of international relations as an academic discipline. Just as Kaunda's efforts at mediation have never been examined in the context of conflict resolution as a discipline (as noted above), so has Zambian foreign policy (surprisingly) never been examined within any part of the broad mainstream of international relations as a discipline. It has been examined within the discipline of a neo-Marxist structuralism. It has been examined in empirical and normative terms. Both camps of examiners have found him wanting - disillusionment in the second camp coming later than in the first, and wondering where the purity has gone. It might be time now to encourage a third perspective on Zambian foreign policy.

A Commonwealth Focus

Since 1982, Zambia has been engaged in a frantic and inconsistent attempt to stave off economic decline. Both party and government have been split on how far IMF measures should be adopted. Technocrats or, often, academics without any public service experience, have been plucked from their usual positions, elevated to positions of responsibility for national finance, and discarded. The sense of improvisation and periodic swings against international fiscal orthodoxy have led various donor - countries to suspend or reduce aid to Zambia. International economic relations are in a mess.

Against this turbulence, Kaunda's interest in sanctions against South Africa, evident from the 1985 Commonwealth summit onwards has been either brave, desperate, or yet another assertion of principle over reality - or a strategy of finely calculated risks that have not yet yielded fruit. The middle 1980s have seen Kaunda use the Commonwealth association increasingly as a vehicle for his foreign policy. There has been a gap here since 1979, when Kaunda hosted the Commonwealth summit in Lusaka which paved the way for the independence of Zimbabwe. Kaunda had worked closely and successfully with the Commonwealth apparatus then, but only returned to it in 1985. His tenure as OAU Chairman in 1987-8 has been marked by his mediatory interventions outside southern Africa. Within his own region, the Commonwealth rather than the OAU has been the instrument of his policy towards South Africa.

Meanwhile, Zambia has not been fully excluded from the increasing hostilities in the region. UNITA staged some border incursions in May 1986; and, at the end of May 1986, a South African air raid struck Zambian targets, purportedly to attack ANC personnel. That air raid, officially admitted by Pretoria, was only the second admitted military action against Zambia in the five years up to 1986. It coincided with attacks against Botswana and Zimbabwe, and were meant as repudiations of the Commonwealth Group of Eminent Persons at that time in South Africa. So far, there have been no signals of a South African attempt to destabilise Zambia by means of a consistent military programme. If nothing else, Kaunda's foreign policy has kept South Africa's military might at arms length. To this extent, the exaggerated nobility and posturing of it all have been successful. To this extent also, it means existing treatments of Zambia's foreign policy and Kaunda's mediatory efforts tend to be unsatisfactory, casting him either as hero or villain. The disentanglement from these two judgements, attempted above, form the narrative outline for my wider study.

PRESIDENTIALISM IN LUSAKA AND HARARE (1989)

You can never go back. That saying is untrue. Sometimes you must go back. What brought me back this time was the need to expunge at last the enigma of Kenneth Kaunda that had haunted my mind ever since I left Zambia in 1985. A research grant had facilitated my visit. (65) I would go to Lusaka first, where I had lived for five years, then Harare, which I knew well. I had first gone to Zimbabwe in January 1980, when it was still Southern Rhodesia, and Lord Soames was the last British Governor, after the death of Smith's regime attempting to hold elections for the independence of the country. A Commonwealth Observer Group was there from January to March, to scrutinise the freeness and fairness of the elections. Attached to the group was a 30 year-old Chinese, hardly daring to remove his dark glasses. Through them, he fell in love with the country and the region. The nearest Commonwealth office was in Lusaka. Later that year he transferred there from London and, amidst great Jacaranda trees, dust and drought, set about having his life changed.

Nine years after, still behind dark glasses, I debouched first at Lusaka International Airport. It's not true that you smell decay. You read it first on hotel menus. Grandly welcomed, I ordered lunch, scanned the prices. Three meals at the third hotel of Lusaka would consume the month's take-home pay of a lecturer at the University of Zambia. I looked up at the waiter. 'How do people survive?' He smiled. They all seem to smile. There had been two popular refrains. The first was, 'we are coping up'. The second, 'oh, but we are suffering here'. The second once had some self-mockery about it. Now, even through a smile, it was the absolute truth.

In the streets around Cairo Road I cut a distinctive figure. The only films in town are rejects from the kung fu circuit. Youngsters loitering outside the cinemas walk up. `We like your Shaolin ponytail.' It's like standing outside the Odeon in

Leicester Square, a Dirty Harry rerun inside, and someone comes up to say you look like Clint Eastwood. I was duly flattered, never carried money in the streets, so I never felt threatened, but insisted always on walking in the open, day or night, rather than barricaded behind the green doors of a Lusaka taxi with the motor and suspension of a tractor.

Public opinion polls are never taken in Zambia. The ruling party, which is the single party, gauges its strength in public rallies where, to be on the safe side, the party faithful and activists are massed, trucked in, given the day off work. The women dance and ululate, though fewer of them now wear the chitenge (traditional wrap-skirt) printed with Kaunda's smiling portrait - the same portrait that's on the bank notes. There's a shortage of dress material. Less shortage of bank notes. The new currency was printed courtesy of Lonhro. As well as the smiling Kaunda, the Freedom Statue of Lusaka is depicted on them. He's tearing chains in two. He stands before what will shortly be the Freedom Plaza, fronting a new Freedom Square, in front of the new Freedom House. The Chinese are building it. Somebody has already tried to burn it down but soon, in Zambia, there will be a Chinese version of the Russian version of praise-architecture. Kaunda will wave his handkerchief from a very high podium, and the party faithful will, from Lusaka's first great square, wave back.

The new currency was introduced at the end of July, 1989, just as I arrived. It included 2 kwacha bills, though K2 buys nothing now. It stopped at K50, which means that, to do the weekly shopping, if you have the wherewithal to shop (if the shops have goods to sell), you carry a large purse, for wallets cannot hold enough notes with which to cope. The party couldn't bear to believe inflation had reached the level it indeed has. A K500 bill would not have been excessive. Almost room here to feel sorry for the elite and wealthy: barrowloads to cart in the K3 million needed for a new Mercedes - probably stolen in South Africa or, if purchased there, paid for by drugs money. Lusaka is the transit route now for Indian narcotics bound for the white boys and girls of South Africa. Ten rand buys one pill of Mandrax. You wash it down with straight whiskey. It has the effect of qualudes - it spaces you out - and it's cheaper. But the Zambian smugglers, thousands of pills in one suitcase, earn enough to buy their cars. The loitering Lusaka youngsters call BMW cars `Buy Mandrax from ...' and then name businessmen and politicians with names that start with W.

All Lusaka, even the party faithful, call the new bank notes 'ninjas'. So that a drink might cost 20 ninja, a hotel meal 360 ninja, a month's pay 1,000 ninja. That's because of the Freedom Statue. He looks like something out of a kung fu film. The broken chains he swirls in the air are the nunchaku, rice flails which, if swung fast enough, can snap a shinbone like a matchstick. In the films, a ninja is a medieval Japanese spy of mythic proportions. He can turn invisible. The Freedom Statue is invisible. The new party headquarters being built behind him are invisible. No one cares. Let the party have its plaza. There will be flooding in Kanyama suburb this year because no one dug the drains. Someone stole the money.

Outside cinemas and bars, I stand with my dark glasses and Shaolin ponytail. I just stand there. People come up and talk. Without knowing it, I am conducting my own, totally random public opinion survey. Each day I stand in another street. Each day more people talk. I collect forty fairly well structured sets of opinion. If Kaunda fell tomorrow, there would be dancing in the streets. I am disturbed by the depth of his unpopularity. He was a hero once. The western world still consider him one. We thought he was a philosopher king and said so in many admiring books.

Perhaps he is still a philosopher king, although he himself would lay less claim now to being a philosopher. His latest book has him professing anguished doubts about his strong-man role. (66) Even in the early 1980s, it seemed written to explain or excuse a slide into personalised government, an absorption of an entire constitution into his being, and his Christian guilt in dispensing sometimes rough justice from an unassailable position. It was too much for his constituency of hitherto loyal supporters in the west. The confession was denounced as too little too late, hypocritical and disingenuous. (67) No, the real problem is that he is a king. He has no challengers. He sees off coup attempts. He centralises everything in himself and in his State House apparatus. Playing golf on private links, he is never far from the phones and advisers that report directly to him. He removes the subsidy from food. He expands the party's Central Committee until it is so large it cannot even be a politburo looking over his shoulder. He addresses the people in the plaza not yet built but, in his mind, the crowd is far below. He is on his high podium and he waves his Turnbull and Asser handkerchief. He cries at the fate of his people like an Olympian who would, if he could by wishing it, by wishing it by himself, turn them all into the unreplenished self-sustaining stars of heaven.

Hair pulled back, dark glasses up front, I walk from office to office. I had many friends here and not one failed to greet me. Those in aid agencies complain their telephones are bugged. Those in the university complain that books, salaries, promotions seem like mirages in their memory. Departments are only half-staffed. There's been a brain-drain to Botswana and Swaziland and, from there, having tasted what it is to purchase once again, scholars hoard against the future when they might find themselves in Zambia, and accept the even more highly-paid faculty positions at bantustan universities. I recall only five years ago, when the glossy South African recruitment leaflets came around, promising much rand, instant professorship for anyone with a Ph.D, everyone greeted them with derision and noble sentiments of a boycott of apartheid. Now, reduced, they are in the bush colleges alongside Ghanaians, Indians . . . all those Pretoria needs to suggest the multi-racialism of the bantustan universities and of the bantustans themselves. But I feel for them. Some of their work was very good. When you're being published in western academic journals, cited by western academics, courted by western editors, but earning enough to buy no more than three meals at a hotel, the same hotel your old friend from the west now stays in, well, life is pretty eroded so why not residual values as well?

Even so, I do not stay long at the university with its great ornamental ponds, its fastidious rows of topiaried flowering shrubs and lines of crimson bougainvillea. While I visit Zambia, de Klerk in South Africa is completing his power struggle against Botha. He says he will talk to Kaunda. I visit many ministers. The cabinet, it seems, are certain Kaunda will refuse to meet de Klerk until after he has won the

South African elections. “We want to see how much support this man has, see what he can deliver." Kaunda, meanwhile, is deciding to meet de Klerk anyway. It takes his ministers by surprised. Kaunda plays to the hilt his image of amazing civility and compassionate understanding. It's all to ensure de Klerk does indeed win the elections. The serious talk will be at another time. This time is just to ensure that the right South African will be at those talks and, moreover, a little in Kaunda's debt. De Klerk is able to portray himself on South African television as a statesman, promising peace in the region. His TV cameras catch him not quite arm-in-arm with a radiantly reasonable black president. In one photo opportunity, Kaunda does tug him by the arm, points with his free hand. ‘Over here is more water.' They're at Victoria Falls. Only the South African (white) and the Zambian (black) heavies ruin the background. They're wearing sunglasses too. It must be 90 in the shade and they, alongside the president and the putative president, are wearing very dark suits. Kaunda is pointing out the water, his handkerchief in hand.

De Klerk, it was said afterwards, devoured ten mountains of briefing paper for his meeting with Kaunda. By contrast, Kaunda received no briefing at all from either his foreign ministry or his party research bureau. He never asked for any and, in any case, they knew precious little about de Klerk. He played it all by ear and pulled it off. He can be a master of this sort of thing, virtuoso of the broad brush stroke, inventor of the Zen of diplomacy. Maybe it's possible in diplomacy. I've always distrusted it, ever since the days of Kissinger and I, then a young student, would wonder how one man in a shuttle could seem to redraw the world. I do not like Olympians. It's my world too. I would like a say in how it's redrawn. All I ever wanted was that an army of foreign policy insurrectionists would spring up, or that a Prometheus of the plebs would saunter into the palace of Olympus and make off with the magic model of the globe.

But, whether or not it is possible in diplomacy, it is not possible in domestic affairs. The nation is suffering immense decline and Kaunda, no economist, and the party seniors who have been with him always, no economists, cannot make the economic beast move forward. Changes in currency, hiring and firing university lecturers as permanent secretaries of finance, endless cabinet reshuffles, fail to address the central issues of too few incentives, too much centralisation, too poor administration, slowly burgeoning corruption and nepotism. The central issues, that is, that can be dealt with. No one can deal with the larger central issues of commodity income, interest rates, and needing the IMF which has, meanwhile, called Zambia's bluff on refusing to meet its conditions with ruthless nonchalance and patience. But, as the squeeze goes on, the president's response is ever more frantic, almost paranoid centralisation. He will gather the nation into State House. There, within the gracious portals of what was once the British Governor's mansion, modelled along the lines of Buckingham Palace, under the last working chandeliers and looking out at the last watered lawns, he and the Zambian people of his imagination will be succored. Safe within the ring of steel he has already put into place. No coup will find him and his familials unprepared.

I left Lusaka armed with catalogues of failure which had been thrust at me. I had hardly tried to obtain them, new grandmaster of the art of interviewing by not interviewing. I had only to enter an office and I would be greeted like an itinerant priest, making house-calls to hear confession. There is growing, let the philosopher-king beware, an immense frustration. It is not that anyone believes in miracle cures, but the sentiment I found from beer-hall, to kung fu cinema, to university, to government offices - everywhere but in the shuttered world of the high party - was that, now, today, this minute, 'somebody else should be allowed to try'. And even members of the high party, giving me lifts in degenerating cars, tyre rods clearly about to rattle off, would turn and say, 'I think, Stephen, I shall be both the first and last generation of my family ever to own a car. The children, if they are honest, will never be able to afford one.' Comrade, perhaps one day soon the children will walk to State House, up past the imaginary Freedom Plaza, along the dusty Independence Avenue, throwing not a single stone upon the lawn of the British Ambassador, and confront the green - uniformed guards with red epaulets outside State House.

Perhaps this will never happen. A more tolerant and peaceful people could scarcely be imagined. But then, not always. I remember one of the times the government closed the university. The students were in the streets, throwing stones and overturning cars. The army came for them in a flying wedge, firing in the air. The students, who had all endured national service, instantly recognised the sound of blank rounds and waded into the soldiers without mercy. These regrouped and charged back, this time with live ammunition. There followed the obligatory tear-gassing and clubbings. But then, as if the nation's entire collection of buses had been mobilised, a fleet of Indian Tata vehicles appeared to take the students to their homes around Zambia where, after all, mothers and fathers still had the right to vote and the party wanted no embarrassments on account of some rowdy youngsters. So, in that curious Zambian combination of stern but ultimately kind parentalism, revolts are put down. But it is the army that puts them down. Only the army can revolt successfully but, already, to forestall this, the generals are ministers, the Prime Minister is a general and, although an amazing military suavity exists in the officer-class, as if everybody had stiffened their lips, learnt their jokes and ritualised their lives at Sandhurst, so that even in civilian suits they seem to carry invisible batons, they could not run the country; and the technocrats have no experience; and the young are too young; and the West, in a 'better the Kaunda we know' mood, sponsors no uprising, nor the South Africans for the same reason, so Kaunda seems from moment-to-moment safe. Centralised. The ninja on the banknotes is a symbol of invisibility, of emptiness. But Kaunda beams out of them, nor has age forgotten his smile, beleaguered, unvictorious, but visible and attempting to spy some inyanga's (witch-doctor's) vision of his perpetual future, and that of his dynasty, clothed in emerald green, astride the in-gathered collapse of the nation.

At the end of the summer, I went to Zimbabwe. There, my most colourful memory was of the Cup Final in the great, circular national stadium, recently built by the Chinese, but featuring a Japanese video replay screen. Two Harare teams, Dynamos and Caps, were battling for the trophy. It was as if Liverpool and Everton made up an all – Mersyside derby, if, by the way, they played at the level of Tranmere Rovers. There was nothing that could remotely pass for midfield play so, perhaps, the Tranmere analogy is misplaced. Wimbledon is more the case. In place of rattles, the capacity crowd waved cow bells but, yes, in the immense heat (so the players must have been really fit), supporters waved the scarves they had worn into the stadium. Unsegregated, I was surrounded by a sea of green or blue. Black and white. If there is one great success of Zimbabwe, it is that colour is no longer an issue. There are, however, other issues, and chief among them is the impending one-party state.

I have never been certain how it happens to me. Perhaps I also have grown invisible, or perhaps I am such a transient visitor, sunglassed in a fortnight's corner, that every cabal on earth can conduct its business and consider my presence not worth a jot. This time in Zimbabwe I found myself in the midst of political dissidents seeking a challenge to the one - party state. Nor have I yet reached the university, where the students support Edgar Tekere's ZUM breakaway party. Because Tekere speaks with a populist ring, with, for the sake of the students, some bland textbook ideologisms. But he is not organising his people well - in part because Mugabe's government won't let him. Every legal and quasi-legal impediment is placed in his path. Every piece of state-owned media ignores his campaign. This is the second martyrdom of Tekere. His first was after he foolishly became associated with an exercise that resulted in the death of a white farmer. Tekere would not make a good president. He has Mugabe's autocratic mien, more charisma, but less intellect and, let's face it, less of that scowling intensity that even hardened western journalists observe hanging about Mugabe like a spiritual cloak. No little man with a moustache, he. But Tekere is manifestly a big man. Despite government efforts, he cannot be dealt out. Alone, however, he cannot really deal himself in. He needs help for that, some form of nation-wide coalition that can be counted upon to cross over tribal lines. He has support among the far-eastern Shona; he has to find a dissident leader among the central Shona; and he has to find people among the Ndebele who resent Nkomo's absorption by Mugabe; he's got to foster a breakaway from Nkomo, get at the root of the horse-trading towards a one-party state but cutting away some of the horses. He must, in short, appeal to tribal chauvinisms, encourage a plethora of small parties, and hope to weld them into a viable opposition, united enough to look credible in Africa's most modern state. The scenario's ridiculous. But that doesn't stop the Harare rumour mills. All manner of prominent names are whispered as being involved. Meanwhile, Mugabe's party moves to patch up its quarrels with exactly these same prominent names. Honorific positions are prepared for them. At each move, rumoured or real, the party checks the dissidents. In the back of my car, one sweltering afternoon on the outskirts of Harare, driving aimlessly near the road to Lusaka, one of the dissidents is swallowing beer and growing animated and, between outbursts in Shona, speaks enough English for me to understand even the detail of what is going on; but, what the hell, the Chinaman is leaving the country soon; the plot is hatched around me and I am, to their intents and purposes, no longer there-a mirage whose hair is flying through the wound-down windows into the day's oven-tinted air.

But, back in the great jacaranda-lined boulevards of the inner city, I am walking past the blind-beggars, past the art galleries, I am making deals with street hucksters for stone sculpture that has fallen off the backs of lorries: because I cannot afford the art-gallery prices; because the sculpture has cliched itself for an international market on the one hand and made itself careless for a tourist market on the other; because it's no longer worth having unless you strike up deals with very knowing sly conmen who have, nevertheless, the eyes of a connoisseur. Because the beggars have always been there for as long as I remember; because they recite from braille Bibles; because one haunting day, as if choreographed, they all read from Saint Matthew and, despite walking from one end of First Street to the other, I got the entire gospel in a seamless sermon that began with meekness and inheritance, and ended with the signs of the last days. Because comrade, I say to the backroom dealer, as he hands over my sculpture, I once risked my life in this country, and I do not think this is what it was for. He smiles, takes my money, courteously waves goodbye to the invisible voice.

I walk down the boulevards, clutching like a weighted rugby ball my sculpture, hand-luggage for the return home. Every second car that speeds past is Japanese and, certainly, every modern car is Japanese. There's a new assembly plant in Willowdale and, thus, the scandal that recently hit the Mugabe-government has been called Willowgate. The intentions were both modest and, in a warped way, upright. Rather than allow politicians to face temptation and become corrupt, it was agreed to make temptation available to them on discount. If every minister could buy a new Japanese car at factory price, he or she would not embezzle funds from ministry budgets to purchase one at retail. A perk would prevent theft. This has worked wonderfully well in Malawi where, as a result, politicians and senior civil servants own half the country - half at least of what is not owned by the President - and all of it was well - gotten; there is no corruption in Malawi. The ruling class got theirs very legally. In the same legal way, Zimbabwean ministers began buying, not just one, but sometimes 20 Japanese cars at factory prices. If they had done this merely to equip their large families, no one would have done more than shrug reasonably resigned shoulders. But, because production is limited, the non-ministerial public must wait for their cars. So the ministers, many now with cars to spare, began selling them at large profits. Some sold so many, earning so much profit, and then took to ordering yet more from the factory that they were in danger of becoming car dealers rather than ministers. The public outcry was immense. Ministers fell. One committed suicide. But the Shaolin ponytail wandering down the boulevards of Harare, was told repeatedly that this was but the tip of an iceberg. At the highest level, corruption is growing. There is afoot a slow ransacking of the country. Its manifestations can be bizarre. The most desirable car in Zimbabwe is neither a BMW nor Mercedes, but a Toyota Cressida - since that was the car at the centre of Willowgate. Meanwhile, if a policeman stops you, don't reach for your wallet. He really does just want to check your indicator and brake lights. You can trust him. The same cannot be said about the Cabinet.

Yet this same Cabinet is not ill-equipped to govern the country. In a very real way it has been an obstacle to Mugabe's presidentialism, his will to make policy by his own fiat. Twice in 1987, it decisively outvoted Mugabe on the question of sanctions against South Africa - on the simple objections that Zimbabweans had already suffered for principle and that sanctions would ruin the country. Yet, the Cabinet was agreed on the dispatch of 10,000 troops to Mozambique - so it is neither quisling nor comprador, nor representative of such a class. But it has sizeable blind spots as well. The war in Mozambique is being wound down to proportions that even the Mozambican government might handle. There are only

3,000 Zimbabwean troops left in the country. The Beira Corridor has attracted immense international investment, including substantial South African investment. When the Zimbabwean troops pull out, there will no longer be a discernible Zimbabwean presence in Mozambique but, Renamo or no Renamo, the South Africans will be there, very deliberately buying up the economy, exchanging one domination for another. Neither the Cabinet nor the President have even requested background papers on the possibility of Zimbabwean investment in the Beira Corridor or in the rest of Mozambique. But, if Zimbabwe doesn't do it, no other frontline state can and, contrary to past form but not contrary to past intentions, Pretoria will eat up Mozambique in a very peaceful way.

There are various Mugabe blind spots like this. Sometimes he seems content with the appearance of progress and not its substance. Until towards the end of his three-year term, he was a most inactive Chairman of the Non-Aligned Movement. In domestic Zimbabwean politics he is concerned so much with the broad brush stroke and so little with the detail, that observers wonder whether he really knows what is going on in the country. Moreover, as in any continual centralisation of broad but definite powers - and these have now been accorded Mugabe under the same constitutional changes that made him President - there will be a growth in the way a single centre attracts flattery and a sanitised version of what is happening beyond the high walls of State House, guarded by its very own neighbouring barracks. With the movement towards a one-party state and, in its wake, the gradual elevation of party policy over Cabinet policy, the President of the country, if he is also president of the party, as in Zambia, will begin to rule alone.

Neither Tekere's ZUM nor any other proposed splinter group look like being successful. The university students are ZUM supporters. While I was in Zimbabwe, Mugabe closed the university. This was for the first time since independence. The last time had been under Smith and several banned students of that period went abroad to take Ph.Ds and became the high-fliers of the new country after their return in 1980. Closure is a symbol that something greater may return. At least it once was. But the campus now is a growing edifice, filled not by an extremely narrow African elite and a wider white representation, but by a growing generation of Zimbabweans who were too young to fight and who were never repressed because of their colour. On the beautiful sloping campus, wooded, the buildings made from brick the colour of terracotta, the students imagine they struggle against an authoritarian government.

They do struggle. They struggle justly but loudly. Their rhetoric is out of proportion to the offence they claim is perpetrated by the government: the embourgoisification of the ruling class. To compare Mugabe to de Klerk is imaginative and ridiculous. Any cool President would have left the students smouldering on their isolated campus, shaking their uncalloused fists at the capitalist sky. But the paternalism of the ruling class, if not bourgeois is immense. The same paternalism has taken Zambia through 25 years now, and close to a brink. The arrogance of rulership that fought for what it has and for what it dispenses in the name of that fight is not to be taken lightly. The struggle is reified, made holy. To be ungrateful is insult enough, but to be ungrateful after never having struggled is sacreligious. Moreover, Mugabe, despite five degrees, never really had a student life. Most of his scholarship was accomplished in prisons. Now to hear the careless insults flowing from the comfortable hill might seem galling.

But to be galled by a few silly words into closing the nation's only university is an over-reaction. Then, to arrest the student leaders; then to arrest their trade union support; then to editorialise about the necessity of it all - the students' lack of proportion is matched well by the government's.

The order to close the campus came from Mugabe. The dissident rumours of Harare, spread by people a dozen times more knowing than the students, are of a President who lives in his own cocoon of power and selected advice; who cannot bear to be slighted or treated below his high station; who cannot bear to feel embarrassment abroad. Thus, with the Commonwealth summit imminent in Kuala Lumpur, it was said that a closed university could not provide criticism of Mugabe, could not embarrass him, while he played the statesman, competed with Kaunda for the morally highest ground. At this time of year, the purple Jacaranda flowers are everywhere on the high trees. When they fall they litter the broad boulevards. Dust rises up and, day by day, it grows hotter. The rain is coming but, first, the heating dust and the thickening of the atmosphere drive people everywhere, not just the blind beggars, to gaze at the sky as if reciting prayers for it finally to rain. In this waterless interregnum passions grow high. Dissidents plot fences for the government, students write amazing pamphlets against the government, and the President coolly buys off the leading figures in the first camp, imperiously, casually sends home like naughty children those in the second. Even his opponents admire his nerve. There is no one else like him in Zimbabwe. Under a one-party state, his lone qualities will quickly be institutionalised. He will be made law. This will not necessarily be to the good. It is not to the good in his northern neighbour.

Driving into Harare, driving into Lusaka, driving into any one of a dozen African capitals, you round a corner. Suddenly, tall white buildings rise from the horizon like sentinels. All over Africa I have sought for the tall grain silos that should rise suddenly in the rural skylines. I do not find them. But I do find the suddenness of cities compelling. One minute we are driving on the road to nowhere. Next, we see the tall, white, symmetrical shafts of concrete and we are cheering in our seats. Because everything is concentrated in them. Nothing happens out of them. Mass is sucked into them. The cities are energised by feeding on all that comes in, until nothing else is left to come in except desultory, dust-laden rumours of rebellion. Overdue, premature, these rumours seek out the last lost Shaolin tourist of Africa, tell him to reduce two icons.

Editors note:

'The Decline of Kaunda: Essays of Praise and Complaint 1983 – 1989' originally appeared (see preface) with an additional chapter: 'The One Party State in Zimbabwe and Zambia (1990-1)'. That essay now appears in revised form in Chapter three: 'Prospects for the 1991 Elections in Zambia'.

Endnotes

(1) Adam Watson, *Diplomacy: the Dialogue between States*, Eyre Methuen, London, 1982, p.170

(2) Oye Ogunbadejo, `Soviet policies in Africa', *African Affairs*, Vol.79, No.316, 1980, pp. 297-299

(3) Adrian Guelke, `Southern Africa and the superpowers', *International Affairs*, Vol. 56, No.4, 1980, p. 651

(4) A.R. Mohamed Babu, `Africa's post- colonial diplomacy', New African, January 1980, p. 39

(5) One of Kissinger's first efforts as National Security Adviser. The NSC report is reprinted in B. Cohen and M.A. El-Khawas, eds, *The Kissinger Study of Southern Africa*, Spokesman Books, Nottingham, 1975

(6) Ibid., pp. 96-97.

(7) Ibid., p. 89

(8) For a good summary, see *New African*, November 1983, p. 49

(9) For a good description of the theory and its decline, see Herbert S. Yee, `The Three World Theory and Post-Mao China's global strategy', *International Affairs*, Vol.59, No.2, 1983

(10) Guelke, op.cit, Ref.3, pp. 657-658

(11) Ogunbadejo, op.cit, Ref.2, p. 309

(12) Timothy M. Shaw, *Dependence and Underdevelopment: The Development and Foreign Policies of Zambia*, Ohio University Centre for International Studies, Athens, Ohio, 1976, pp.v and 54

(13) Timothy M. Shaw, `Zambia: dependence and underdevelopment', *Canadian Journal of African Studies*, Vol.X, No.1, 1975. Shaw's line is very much an expression of dependency theory.

(14) For example, Marcia Burdette, `The political economy of Zambian foreign policy, 1970-80', *Journal of Southern African Studies*, April 1984

(15) William Tordoff, `Zambia: the politics of disengagement', *African Affairs*, Vol.76, No.302, 1977, p.69

(16) Ibid, p.68

(17) Douglas Anglin, `Zambia and Southern African liberation movements: 1964-1974', in Timothy M. Shaw and Kenneth A. Heard, eds., *The Politics of Africa: Dependence and Development*, Longman, London, 1979, p.184

(18) Ibid, pp.199 and 201

(19) Timothy M. Shaw, `The foreign policy of Zambia: ideology and interests', *The Journal of Modern African Studies*, Vol.14, No.1, 1976

(20) Jan Pettman, *Zambia: Security and conflict,* Julian Friedman, Lewes, 1974

(21) Graham Mytton, `Review of Pettman', *African Affairs*, Vol.74, No.294, 1975, pp.111- 112

(22) For a good discussion of this problem throughout Africa, see Zdenek Cervenka, ed. *Landlocked Countries of Africa*, Scandinavian Institute of African Studies, Uppsala, 1973

(23) Simon Katzenellenbogen, `Zambia and Rhodesia: pioneers of the past-a note on the history of railway politics in Central Africa', *African Affairs*, Vol.73, No.290, 1974

(24) Guy Arnold and Ruth Weiss, *Strategic Highways of Africa*, Julian Friedmann, London, 1977, p.163

(25) Deon Geldenhuys, *The Diplomacy of Isolation: South African Foreign Policy Making*, Macmillan for the South African Institute of International Affairs, Johannesburg, 1984, p.153

(26) *Ibid*, footnote 194, pp. 271-272

(27) A note of caution here: Smith closed the border in 1973 to stimulate publicity after a border incident. Ten hours later, he proposed to exempt copper from his closure; three weeks later, he proposed to lift the closure entirely. Zambia refused to accept this reversal, claiming Smith was ``too hostile a neighbour''. By the end of 1974, however, Zambia was found to be using Rhodesian railways for various copper movements to Mozambican ports. See Arnold and Weiss, op cit, Ref.24, pp.78 and 127. However, a full and free flow of traffic through Rhodesia to South African ports had to await 1978.

(28) Gendenhuys, op cit, Ref.25, pp.229-230

(29) Robert M. Price, `Pretoria's Southern African strategy', *African Affairs*, Vol.83, No.330, 1984. For an earlier view, see also James Barber, *South Africa's Foreign policy 1945-1970*, Oxford University Press, 1973. In the present author's view, the best recent analysis of South African foreign policy is Gendenhuys, op cit, Ref.25.

(30) For my view of the importance of personalities in Commonwealth summitry, see Stephen Chan, `Three birds of different feathers: the Commonwealth, the Commonwealth Secretary-General and the Commonwealth Secretariat', *The Round Table*, No.291, 1984.

(31) Much has already been written on the prospects for SADCC. For a reasonable, dispassionate account, see Christopher R. Hill, 'Regional co- operation in Southern Africa', *African Affairs*, Vol.82, No.327, 1983. For an optimistic account, see Douglas Anglin, 'Economic integration in Southern Africa', *International Organisation*, Autumn 1983.

(32) Fergus MacPherson, *Kenneth Kaunda of Zambia*, Lusaka: Oxford University Press, 1974

(33) e.g. as in Richard Hall, *The High Price of Principles: Kaunda and the White South*, London: Hodder and Stoughton, 1969.

(34) Stephen Chan, 'Lusaka or Harare?', *NZ International Review*, vol.X, no.2, 1985.

(35) e.g. Bastiaan de Gaay Fortman (ed.), *After Mulungushi - The Economics of Zambian Humanism,* Nairobi: East Africa Publishing House, 1969.

(36) For an overview of Zambia's development problems, see Ben Turok (ed.), *Development in Zambia*, London: Zed Press, 1979

(37) For a discussion, see Gatian F. Lungu, *Administrative Decentralisation in the Zambian Bureaucracy*, Lusaka: Institute for African Studies, 1985.

(38) See Muna Ndulo and Kaye Turner, *Civil Liberties Cases in Zambia*, Oxford: African Law Reports, 1984

(39) Two recent biographies of Kaunda's greatest opponents could be published because their subjects were dead. Even so, the record of their opposition was not censored. Goodwin Mwangilwa, *Harry Mwaanga Nkumbula-a biography of the 'old lion' of Zambia*, Lusaka: Multimedia, 1982; and Goodwin Mwangilwa, *The Kapwepwe Diaries*, Lusaka: Multimedia, 1986.

(40) Particularly by Timothy Shaw. See Douglas Anglin and Timothy M. Shaw, *Zambia's Foreign Policy: Studies in Diplomacy and Dependency*, Boulder, Colorado: Westview, 1979

(41) For a summary of my views on this, see Stephen Chan, `The Search for Peace - the basis of Zambia's regional policy', *Contemporary Review*, vol.248, no.1444, 1986

(42) To be published from London by I.B. Tauris. The research has attracted a grant from the British Economic and Social Research Council and this is gratefully acknowledged.

(43) One of the first-fruits of that period was Timothy M. Shaw, *Dependence and Underdevelopment: The Development and Foreign Policies of Zambia*, Athens Ohio: Ohio University Centre for International Studies, 1976.

(44) In 1976 alone, apart from the Ohio monograph *ibid*., Timothy M. Shaw, `Zambia: Dependence and Underdevelopment', *Canadian Journal of African Studies*, Vol.X, No.1, 1976; `The Foreign Policy of Zambia: Ideology and Interests', *The Journal of Modern African Studies*, Vol.14, No.1, 1976. In 1979, he published his major statement on Zambian foreign policy: Douglas Anglin and Timothy M. Shaw, *Zambia's Foreign Policy: Studies in Diplomacy and Dependency*, Boulder Colorado: Westview, 1979; and also began writing on dependency outside southern Africa. Timothy M. Shaw and Kenneth A. Heard (eds.), *The Politics of Africa: Dependence and Development*, London: Longman and Dalhousie University Press, 1979. In the decades since then, there has been an almost annual output of mostly edited volumes on the theme of dependency throughout Africa.

(45) e.g. Marcia M. Burdette, `The Mines, Class Power, and Foreign Policy in Zambia', *Journal of Southern African Studies*, Vol.10, No.2, 1984.

(46) See Stephen Chan, *Issues in International Relations - A View from Africa*, London: Macmillan, 1987; and also Stephen Chan, *Exporting Apartheid: Foreign Policies in Southern Africa*, London: Macmillan, 1990.

(47) All in the Heinemann African Writers series (London). Dominic Mulaisho's *Tongue of the Dumb*, 1971, was considerably more successful than his *Smoke that Thunders*, 1979, even though the latter is a rendition of white settler rebellion in a parody of Rhodesia. Kaunda's *Zambia Shall be Free*, 1962, is autobiographical rather than fictional.

(48). Kenneth Kaunda (and Colin Morris) *Black Government? A Discussion*, London: United Society for Christian Literature, 1960; *A Humanist in Africa - Letters to Colin Morris*, London: Longman, 1966; (ed. Colin Morris) *Kaunda on Violence*, London: Collins, 1980; among others.

(49) Richard Hall, *The High Price of Principles: Kaunda and the White South*, London: Hodder and Stoughton, 1969. A very fair and objective account of Zambia's policy towards UDI in Rhodesia and links with South Africa, detailing both principles and pragmatism, mistakes and vacillation, is found in Sam C. Notlutshungu, *South Africa in Africa: A study of ideology and foreign policy*, Manchester: Manchester University Press, 1975, pp.218- 258.

(50) e.g. Bastiaan de Gaay Fortman (ed.), *After Mulungushi - The Economics of Zambian Humanism*, Nairobi: East African Publishing House, 1969.

(51) e.g. Fergus MacPherson, *Kenneth Kaunda of Zambia*, Lusaka: Oxford University Press, 1974; John Hatch, *Two African Statesmen*, London: Secker and Warburg, 1976; Richard Hall, *Kaunda, Founder of Zambia*, London: Longman, 1964.

(52) For a description of the three world theory, see Herbert S. Yee, `The Three World Theory and Post-Mao China's global strategy', *International Affairs*, Vol.59, No.2, 1983. For a consideration of its romantic bias and cultural base, see

Stephen Chan, `China's Foreign Policy and Africa: The Rise and Fall of China's Three World Theory', *The Round Table*, No.296, 1985. Curiously, for a theory of international relations that revised the idea of multi-polarity, and which was advanced by a major power, it received scant critical attention in the west. An exception was provided by Peter Worsley, `One World or Three? A Critique of the World-system Theory of Immanuel Wallerstein', in R. Miliband and J. Saville (eds.) *Socialist Register, 1980*, London: Merlin Press,1980.

(53) Mwizenge Tembo gave *Kaunda on Violence* a polite review, *The Journal of Modern African Studies*, Vol. 19, No.2, 1981, but even he noted Kaunda's slide from idealism to despair. Otherwise, the book was either studiously ignored in the academic press or given excoriating reviews. See, e.g., R.V. Sampson's review in *African Affairs*, Vol.81, No.325,1982.

(54) See Muna Ndulo and Kaye Turner, *Civil Liberties Cases in Zambia*, Oxford: The African Law Reports, 1984; see also Lawrence Zimba, *Zambian Bill of Rights*, Nairobi: East African Publishing House, 1984.

(55) See Section 2.`X is for the Eagle.'

(56) 'Humanism, Intellectuals and the left in Zambia', See Section 4

(57) See Section 5, `Kaunda as international casualty'.

(58) See Kwaku Osei-Hwedie and Muna Ndulo, op. cit.; William Tordoff, *Politics in Zambia*, Manchester: Manchester University Press 1974; Tordoff, *Administration in Zambia*, Manchester University Press, 1980. For the rise of the party, see Ian Scott, *Party Politics in Zambia: a study of the organisation of UNIP*, unpublished Ph.D of the University of Toronto, 1976; and B.C. Chikulo, `The Zambia Administrative Reforms: An Alternative View', *Public Administration and Change*, Vol.1, No.1, 1981. For the difficulties of decentralisation, see Gatian F. Lungu, *Administrative Decentralisation in the Zambian Bureaucracy*, Lusaka: Institute for African Studies , 1985.

(59) For his autobiography, see Vernon Mwaanga, An Extraordinary Life, and The Other Society, both London: Fleetwood Publishers, 1984 and 1987.

(60) Guy Arnold and Ruth Weiss, *Strategic Highways of Africa*, London: Julian Friedmann, 1977, pp.78 and 127.

(61) Deon Geldenhuys, *The Diplomacy of Isolation - South African Foreign Policy Making*, Johannesburg: Macmillan, 1984, pp.271-2, footnote 194.

(62) Kaunda's hopes for UNITA were taken by Timothy M. Shaw's first editors as proof of Kaunda's comprador-ism. See the editors' foreword to Timothy M. Shaw, *Dependence and Underdevelopment: The Development and Foreign Policies of Zambia*, op. cit. Shaw himself was nowhere so specific or crude.

(63) William Tordoff, `Zambia: the Politics of Disengagement', *African Affairs*, Vol.76, No.302, 1977, p.68.

(64) For a very fine account of aspects of the work of the Contact Group, see Vivienne Jabri, `The Western Contact Group as Intermediary in the Conflict over Namibia', in C.R. Mitchell and Keith Webb (eds.), *New Approaches to International Mediation*, Westport, Connecticut: Greenwood Press, 1988; and for a more extended account by the same author *Mediating Conflict: Decision- making and Western intervention in Namibia*, Manchester University Press, 1990.

(65) A grant from the Economic and Social Research Council, to prepare a book entitled, *Kaunda and Southern Africa: Image and Reality in Foreign Policy.*

(66) Kenneth Kaunda (ed. Colin Morris), *Kaunda on Violence*, London: Collins, 1980.

(67) Especially the review by R.V. Sampson in *African Affairs*, Vol.81, No.325, 1982.

PART II

CHAPTER TWO

PROSPECTS FOR THE 1991 ELECTIONS IN ZAMBIA (1991)

I thought I would start the discussion this evening by a prognosis about what might happen if indeed there is a change of government in Zambia after October this year and what might happen if there is a government led by Frederick Chiluba, the current head of the Movement for Multi-party democracy. There would be quite a different government to what currently pertains in Zambia.

First of all I would like to give you some background about Frederick Chiluba. The name is spelt CHILUBA, but in fact the 'b` is a silent or slurred 'b', so if he does become the next president of Zambia, then the correct pronunciation is Chilua. He is a trade unionist, not a technocrat at all, but somebody with a firebrand past. A lot of this firebrand image has now been very well contained, because most of the other senior members of the Movement for Multi-party Democracy are highly qualified technocrats. A high number of businessmen are in the upper party echelons and also a surprising number of very fine constitutional lawyers. In fact, this representation of constitutional lawyers in the MMD has been responsible, to a very large extent, for the success of its campaigns so far. What has happened in the campaign is that the Kaunda party, the ruling party, has tried its best to throw all kinds of impediments in the way of free campaigning; one by one the impediments have been challenged in the courts and have been defeated and this has been made possible by the strong legal presence already mentioned.

Although Chiluba with his firebrand image is leading the opposition party, he is very well advised and has a technocratically orientated and well run opposition party and I think it could be a reasonably well run government. Chiluba himself has a popular base in Zambia, not only amongst his own Bemba people and the mining community of which he was a major trade union leader, but in the community as a whole. He is a very short person, so there is a very great physical contrast between himself and Kaunda. Kaunda as you know is a very large person who is physically very imposing. At one point in the early 1980s, when I was living in Zambia, there was a contretemps between Kaunda and Chiluba. At that point the President tried to demean Chiluba by referring to the fact that he is so small. He only just clears about 5 ft. and at that point the President tried to insult him by asking how a man who is only 4 ft.2 could aspire to lead a country like Zambia. This was followed immediately by major demonstrations in the streets with people chanting slogans and carrying placards saying '6 ft.4 out; 4 ft.2 in'. These things were turned to advantage by an even then embryonic opposition movement.

What I want to talk about this evening is to give a history of how the opposition movement grew; how suddenly it took off, really only about a year ago, in six very packed months.

I will say a few things about what it means for the region and then give my prognosis as to what is going to happen in the election. Should an MMD government come to power, I think the immediate effect, as far as this country is concerned, would be a vast loosening of what have been difficulties in terms of trade and other economic interchange. There will be a very great and very urgently felt demand for high investment levels, for liquidity inputs. I think that you will find South Africa being very positively and enthusiastically courted by a new government - it would be very anxious indeed for investment and I will say more about that in due course.

If there is a new government composed of businessmen, people who believe in a free market, people who populate a very small, but highly specialized, private sector in Zambia - if these people become government, there will be a significant change from the sort of relationships South Africa has had with Zambia in the past.

If you look at past relationships - and this has been one not only of confrontation and rhetorical condemnation on the part of President Kaunda towards South African governments - you have also had, I think, a fairly well structured intellectual conception of what foreign policy should be. In other words, if you were looking at the region from a Zambian point of view, then the Zambians viewed the region as if some form of balance of power held sway - a balance of power in which there were two poles of power - the South Africans very obviously being one, but also the Zambians acting as a counter-weight, a countervailing pole of power in the region.

At first glance this seems ridiculous, because South Africa is clearly an economic and military giant and alongside that Zambia is puny. The concept as far as the Zambians were concerned was that you did indeed have a pole of economic and military power here in South Africa, but what Kaunda and the Zambians tried to confront that with was an opposite pole of legitimacy - in particular, moral legitimacy. This is what lay behind the President's constant talking about man's inherent goodness; about Christian and humanist approaches to international relations; and lay behind his international image, which he assiduously cultivated, of being a peace-maker, a mediator and negotiator. Everywhere he went, he portrayed this very carefully calculated image of himself as a peaceful man interested in talk rather than war. It was carefully cultivated not just as an image in its own right and for its own sake, but to contrast with what he tried to portray as a bellicose, unreasonable foreign policy emanating from South Africa. He tried to emphasize Zambia as a moral counter-weight to a militaristic and an economic heavy-weight power here in South Africa.

It was with that sort of balance in mind that he became the only Front-line President ever to hold direct, face-to-face talks with South African leaders and there have been three such Summit meetings in the history of the relationships between the two countries. If you consider the last four leaders there has been a relationship of one sort or another. Even under the Verwoerd government, although there was never any formal meeting between the two leaders, there was a very great deal of correspondence.

The Zambian point of view was one of opposition to apartheid in this country, but also one where communication and perhaps negotiation could be possible. So when Prime Minister Vorster took office, there was a very concerted movement on his part to try and open up some sort of dialogue with Kaunda. There were several on-off, start-stop attempts to make these talks work, until finally in 1975 there was a famous meeting between the two men and Ian Smith along with the nationalist leaders of Rhodesia, now Zimbabwe, on the Victoria Falls bridge. That was the first Summit meeting between a Zambian leader and a South African leader - a meeting that was not exactly approved by other members of the southern African community. There were various limitations placed upon Kaunda. President Nyerere of Tanzania had firm words to say on just how far Kaunda could go in these talks - how much he could concede and how much he could not concede.

After the independence of Zimbabwe, there was another Summit meeting, this time in Botswana between President Kaunda and Prime Minister Botha. The meeting discussed all kinds of regional issues. Although the Zambian President has half-heatedly in his press releases tried to claim credit for instigating the train of thought that led to the Nkomati Accord and the Lusaka Accord of 1984, they probably were not discussed in formal terms at the time. It was very much an attempt to establish common ground for negotiation instead of bloodshed in the region. Prime Minister Botha went to that meeting very well briefed as to Kaunda's predilections and his own approach to negotiations. It was Botha himself who asked Kaunda, since he was meant to be a peaceful and religious man, to open those talks with prayer. In other words, this view of Kaunda as a person wearing his moral heart on his sleeve was something that the South African Prime Minister was well briefed about and that he sought to exploit.

I want to come back to this idea of being well briefed about Kaunda and to contrast that with how Kaunda prepares for Summit meetings himself. Of course, what you have had in more recent times, in fact very shortly after President de Klerk took office as State President, was a meeting at Victoria Falls between Presidents de Klerk and Kaunda. Again, I will come back to that to illustrate my point about briefing and preparation.

What has happened in the last decade and a half is that various contacts were made between the Zambians and the South Africans. These were contacts that Kaunda and Zambia were able to make because there was no countering force within the Front-line States saying that he could not make them. Nyerere could try to impose limits, but effectively, in geographic terms, Tanzania was not really a member of the Front-line. Zambia was directly in the front-line. There was nobody of comparable stature to put really effective limitations on what Kaunda might try to do by way of foreign policy.

All of that changed after 1980. With the advent of an independent Zimbabwe, what you had - and this is quoting the last American ambassador to Harare, when I was speaking to him a couple of years ago - was "that what Mugabe has is a real state, he has a real economy, he has got a real army" - in other words if you look at the region since 1980 then a state with some muscle had arrived. This was muscle that Kaunda never had. He knew he never had it, which is why he always tried to contrive a moral image in place of the sort of muscle that Zimbabwe was later able to have. If you have two states in the region trying to mount some sort of challenge to Pretoria and with different bases of strength - in Zimbabwe's case a real economic infrastructure, then what is going to happen is a competition between two of the front-line states. This is precisely what happened - a great rivalry developed between Kaunda and Mugabe. On the surface they went out of their way to portray a united front-line approach to the region and its problems; underneath the surface a great deal of rivalry, sometimes a bitter rivalry, developed. Now, I think that the situation is starting to change again, because with the recent independence of Namibia, with the prospects for the winding-down of conflict and elections next year in Angola - what you are going to have if you take Zimbabwe and Namibia and Angola - will be three regional states with genuine economic and resource bases. In other words, if you draw a map of the poles of power - even of economic power - in the southern African region in the year 2000, than what southern Africa is going to look like is very different indeed from what it looks like now.

Even if Kaunda survives the forthcoming elections, what it means is that the region is becoming more and more populated with serious actors and he can no longer count on being accepted as spokesperson for the region. Over the last ten years, since Zimbabwe's independence, this position of spokesperson has been under heavy challenge. The Zimbabweans want very much to play a leading role in the region.

The distrust between Zimbabwe and Zambia I will come back to in the context of the preparations that Kaunda made to meet with de Klerk, shortly after de Klerk became State President. I would like to say just a few words about how Kaunda currently stands, not just amongst the Front-line States, but amongst the great powers. I think that if you look, for instance, at the relationship that now pertains between Zambia and the United States, it is a strange relationship indeed. Coming back to the Front-line States, if there is one of their members in good books with the United States right now, then it is Zimbabwe. The U.S. was very happy indeed with the Zimbabwean chairmanship of the Security Council and how helpful they were over the Gulf crisis: when the Iraq conflict blew up there was a need to build a United Nations-based coalition to confront what was happening in the Gulf area, the Zimbabweans were having their turn as President of the Security Council and they did everything that the Americans wanted them to do. They delivered and the Americans were extremely happy. If, in future years, you find that the Americans are supporting their Minister of Finance, Bernard Chidzero for the Secretary-Generalship at the United Nations, then that is the pay-off for the constructive help that the Zimbabweans gave. Conversely the Americans were furious with Kaunda. You might remember seeing on CNN News that the last statesman to get to Baghdad before the bombs fell was Kaunda. Ostensibly he was on a peace-keeping, mediating mission. But it certainly didn't come across as such. He was seen walking down Baghdad streets arm in arm with President Saddam. When that happened, apparently, the telephone lines, the telex lines, the fax lines were burning red-hot between Washington and the American Embassy in Lusaka. I am not sure I can repeat exactly what these cables said in polite company, but I can give you some indication - they went along the lines of "What the ... is this ... doing walking down a Baghdad street with Saddam?" Apparently for something like 18 hours this constant bombardment of inquiries from Washington was bouncing off the desks of the harassed American embassy staff in Lusaka, who could only reply: "We don't know what he is doing there. No one knows what he is doing there."

'No one knows what Kaunda is doing there' : that is a theme I would like to have a look at right now. I said I would refer briefly to Kaunda and the Front-line States in the context of the de Klerk meeting. I was in Zambia at the time this happened and I know for a fact that the Foreign Minister didn't know that Kaunda was going to meet de Klerk; the Deputy Foreign Minister didn't know that he was going to meet de Klerk; nobody in the Cabinet knew that he was going to meet with de Klerk; the entire Foreign Service - the Ministry of Foreign Affairs - didn't know that he was going to meet de Klerk; nobody in the Central Committee of the ruling party knew that he was going to meet de Klerk - until shortly before it all happened! It was announced in the papers and of course you know the consequences of what happened here in terms of the power struggle between Botha and de Klerk. What happened in Zambia is that everybody just sat around with their mouths open, saying (in effect) "Well we didn't know that he was going to meet de Klerk!" Afterwards I spoke to some of his senior people and asked: 'How did Kaunda prepare for his meeting with de Klerk?' and they said 'Well we understand that de Klerk was probably briefed every hour on the hour about Kaunda, but Kaunda asked for no briefing at all. Then I went to the Ministry of Foreign Affairs and asked the people there "Can I see your file, your profile, your background material on de Klerk?" and they said "We don't have a file on de Klerk. He was the last man on earth we expected to become the State President of South Africa. In any case, even if we had a file on de Klerk, it would never have been requested by State House. We do what State House, what the President asks us to do. We don't make inputs of this sort. We don't have a policy role. If he had even told us that he was going to meet with de Klerk, he wouldn't have asked us for assistance in that particular meeting."

If you take the question of consultation on how to act outside Zambia and you discuss how Kaunda approached the Front-line States on this particular matter, apparently there was a Front-line Summit shortly before this meeting - all of the Presidents of the Front-line States got together in Harare for one of their regular summits - and I talked to Zimbabwean Foreign Affairs people who were present as aides to president Mugabe at this particular summit - their recollection was very much that right at the end of the meeting, under 'any other business' Kaunda suddenly announced - it wasn't a consultation - 'Incidentally I propose to meet with de Klerk in about two weeks from now.' As you can imagine, there was consternation among the other front-line Presidents - 'How can you do this; why are you not consulting us, why are you just telling us?' The upshot of that was that they decided to rein in Kaunda saying that he could go and meet de Klerk, as President of Zambia, but in no way as a representative of the Front-line. So the Front-line disassociated itself from that particular meeting - it became solely a President to President summit.

What I am trying to get at here is the way that he makes policy. It is very much spur-of-the-moment; it is often crisis-driven, in other words he likes nothing better than a crisis to respond to. If you are thinking in terms of long term-term forward or strategic planning, then there is very little of that in Foreign Affairs. If he divines that a moment is right for a certain action, he will follow that intuition. What all this is getting to is that if he behaves this way in foreign policy, does he behave exactly in this way when it comes to domestic policy? The answer is: 'Yes, he does.' Because he behaves this way in domestic policy, it goes some way towards explaining the chronic and social mess that Zambia is in right now.

I want to draw a very firm distinction between Kaunda's idiosyncratic behavior and the expertise that is available in Zambia. In other words if the civil service had been called upon to assist in policy making, if the technocratic community or the academic community had been called upon to assist with policy making, then you would see a very different policy coming out of Lusaka. But because this assistance is not built into the Zambian governing structure, because everything comes out of State House on an intuitive, spur-of-the-moment basis, a great deal of Confusion exists in Zambian domestic policy. There are competing factions within the Zambian Civil service, particularly on economic matters, but because the President is not himself an economist and doesn't actually understand economic matters very well, this means first that he is not able to arbitrate effectively between the different approaches to the country's economic problems and secondly it means that he is not able to take a coherent and cogent lead in economic matters - "here is a crisis, let's try to grapple with that crisis only in terms of that crisis and not in terms of its deeper implications and certainly not in terms of the long-term problems of Zambia, its future development and debt repayments. None of this is properly addressed; none of it has a strategic planning base.

What this has meant over the years is that Zambia has drifted from economic crisis to economic crisis, creating certain difficulties in the Zambian position with regard to the international donor community. There are something like eight million people in Zambia officially. I think that is an under-estimate, the number is closer to ten million, but the debt is to the tune of seven billion US dollars. Even if you take ten million people as a base, this makes it the largest indebted nation in the world on a per capita basis. In other words, nowhere else in the world do people owe more money per head than in Zambia. When you look at this figure of seven billion, there are two obvious comments. The first is that the debt figure hasn't actually risen very much in the last ten years - what has declined is Zambia's capacity to keep up its payments - so that is where the crisis stems from, an incapacity to keep up payments, not a gigantic increase in debt. The second comment is that it reflects only the official debt. If you calculate in also the unofficial debt - and by that I mean items not co - ordinated in terms either of the Ministry of Finance or the Reserve Bank of Zambia, but individual, independent deals and arrangements made by individual industries, government parastatals, etc., then that figure is probably considerably larger. No one knows how to start calculating exactly what that debt would be, but even at the total official debt of seven billion, there is no real prospect of being able to pay it or even being able to keep up the service payments.

This means all kinds of dislocations - not only in economic planning but in terms of services and infrastructure provisions for the citizens of Zambia. Nothing works Right now – the hospital is rationed to 2 hours of water a day - this is the major hospital and the university teaching hospital. Running a very large medical enterprise like that with 2 hours of running water a day - you can imagine how horrific the situation is. The families of the patients there not only have to bring in food for their relatives, but in fact have to scour the black market themselves for medical supplies, even down to dressings and bandages, never mind drugs. The situation is desperate. As you know, there is a cholera epidemic, again related to this question of a lack of water supply, and in fact the water hasn't been treated for something like six years. All of these years of neglect are catching up with the country because there is no infrastructural input. There is no money by which infrastructural input can be afforded. because of the inability to meet payments on time, and to service the international debt, the donor countries have become more and more reluctant to advance credit or to give money to Zambia.

All of this has had repercussions in terms of the electorate. I have monitored three Zambian elections and have always been very surprised by the sophistication of the Zambian electorate. If it was possible to do a formal opinion survey, to do a poll in Zambia - it is not possible, but if it were - then I would suspect that you would get a large number of extremely intelligent replies from the electorate at large, even on a completely random basis. In the election coming up, I think that they know what they are voting for and I don't think that they are so naive as to think that any problems that they might have can be addressed overnight - that there are going to be any sudden improvements in their standards of living, because manifestly this is not going to be the case with all kinds of deeply imbedded structural problems which have to be sorted out. But I think that the Zambians will know that what they are voting for is the concept of change and the constitutional guarantee of change. I think that they are going to exercise that electoral right to impose change in terms of the government of their own destinies.

The history of it all really is only a year and a bit old. In March last year, Kaunda - and here is an example of how out of touch he was with his electorate - in March last year he proposed 14 constitutional amendments to Parliament. These constitutional amendments - all 14 of them - were designed to increase his power as President and to increase the power of the single party, the single party state.

Already by this time there was significant dissatisfaction, not only within the electorate, but within the ruling party itself. Kaunda was unable to muster the 2/3 majority that was needed in parliament to pass these constitutional amendments. In fact not only was he unable to muster the 2/3 majority in parliament that he needed, what the introduction of the fourteen constitutional amendments did was to foment a back-bench revolt. This back-bench revolt came to a head at the fifth national convention of the ruling party.

For the first time at one of these major party gatherings, something which had the same importance for the ruling party as for instance the ANC congress in Durban had for South African politics here, people got up and made speeches opposing government policy and opposing what the president was trying to do. This was a significant breakthrough.

What this did was to put Kaunda into a panic, so that by May 1990, under pressure, he suddenly announced that there was going to be a referendum the following August. It was to be on the possibility of a multi-party state in Zambia. In other words, after his misjudgment over constitutional amendments and all the furore within his own party that this occasioned, he suddenly conceded the principle of pluralism and said that there was going to be a referendum - in August 1990 - in which the multi-party state became a possibility. What happened however was that by the time he got around to June of 1990, under pressure from the IMF, Kaunda decided to remove subsidy levels from the basic food of the Zambian people. This meant was that something in the order of 100% and 140% rises in the price of mealies was occasioned. This caused riots in the streets of Lusaka. These riots quickly involved not only the ordinary citizens of Lusaka, but also the university students and, within 24 hours it also involved the armed forces in Zambia. The armed forces at this time had not planned a coup. It was very much a spontaneous, an extemporaneous approach to replace the government. Although the official Zambian position was that it was just a single deranged signal lieutenant, who single-handedly occupied the broadcasting complex in Lusaka, I think that one doesn't have to dig very deeply to find out that it was a significant, very hastily, but a significant hastily organized coup attempt on the part of a number of junior officers.

When I was giving an interview on Radio South Africa the number of security checks that we had to go through before we actually reached the studio, was quite impressive. You have to do the same sort of thing to get into the Zambian broadcasting network, so that the idea of one lieutenant, which is the official Zambian line, storming the broadcasting complex by himself, holding himself on the air, ordering everybody at bay on his own and then broadcasting without a technician or any technical support while keeping all the support and electrical services operating, is obviously far fetched. In fact the fire-fight that followed when loyal government forces retook the station left something like 19 soldiers dead. There were at least two or three platoons of supporting soldiers holding out with that particular lieutenant, enough to hold the station for several hours.

People were in the streets celebrating, several Land-Rovers of soldiers were in the suburbs announcing that Kaunda had fallen and now was the time to rejoice and the people did indeed rejoice and dance in the streets. Kaunda put down this particular revolt. He put down this particular coup attempt because it had been so hastily organized. He put it down, but he realised by this stage that public opinion was very much against him. He tried to mollify public opinion by a number of measures and the subsidies went back on the maize staple food very quickly; everyone involved in that particular coup attempt was pardoned in the next month; all of the protagonists of the last two coup attempts before then were also pardoned.

He still needed a breathing space and he realised that if he went to the nation in August with a referendum for a multi-party state, the people would probably say "Okay, let's have a multi-party state and let's have elections right away." The breathing space Kaunda wanted was considerably longer. In July he postponed the referendum and in September said that there was not going to be any referendum at all and in one year's time - this October - without there being any referendum, there would be direct elections. Any party would be able to contest the elections. In other words he conceded that there had to be a multi-party state, he didn't bother to go through a referendum process. What he wanted was one year to prepare himself and his party to be competitive if an election took place. What has happened in a year, as I have said, is that the government has tried to put every impediment possible in the path of the opposition. But the opposition because of its legal expertise, has been able to challenge these impediments in the courts and has won a string of victories through the legal process. Their rallies are particularly well attended and if you were to do a head count comparison between the sort of numbers that Kaunda and his members get on the hustings and the sort of numbers that the multi-party movement is getting, then it is the MMD that is leading right now.

The major card that Kaunda is playing however, is the very suspect background of some of these leading lights in the multi-party movement. If you are trying to sustain yourself as a business man in Zambia's economic climate, then what you need to do in order to survive as a business man is to behave in ways sometimes not entirely lawful and indeed a great deal of the venture capital which these people have succeeded in raising to put into their legitimate businesses has come through illegitimate means. (Since this meeting is on the record, I won't say who is involved, but it has its own Johannesburg connection. You might be worried by the drug market in this city, particularly in the barbiturate drugs, which has a sort of qualude effect, I think you call it Mandrex down here. It is available in lots of the discotheques and drinking parlours in the city. Most of the Mandrax which finds its way into Johannesburg is manufactured, in the first place, in India, in third world chemical laboratories, and Lusaka is the major trans-shipment point.)

When it suits government, it keeps quiet about these things, but because it now suits them to try and expose the murky backgrounds of some of these businessmen who are leading the movement for multi-party democracy, a lot of this is now being brought out into the open. There is a great deal of mud-slinging, of accusations - that "they are more corrupt than we are, etc, etc." - not "we are more honest than they are: - that has long gone by the wayside in Zambian electoral politics - but: "Yes they have uncovered evidence that we have got Swiss bank accounts, but their bank accounts are larger than ours". This is the sort of back-biting, the sort of dirty trickery that is now taking place in Zambian electoral politics, which makes it very interesting. If you want to compile a dossier with which to blackmail your future partners from that country you only have to spend a month or so in Zambia and listen to the electoral hustings. I won't make any further comment about that.

Let me give you some international opinions about what is going to happen and then close by saying what I think is going to happen in these elections. I should point out that there are going to be two elections. One for Parliament and one for the Presidency. The Americans at this stage think that Kaunda could just shade the Presidency - maybe just win the election - but he would have to deal with a parliament very firmly in control of the MMD. In other words, the current opposition will control Parliament, but with Kaunda still as President.

Kaunda, from my information, is prepared to accept a situation like that. Because what he has been angling for is a new constitutional base, very much along French lines, which gives the President power over and above what parliament can do. It may mean ditching all of his lieutenants and supporters in his UNIP party but he is prepared to do that, if it means that he is able to hang onto personal power. The Americans think that this is a possibility, that there could be this division of power in Zambia. The Americans are not alone in this particular point of view but the British are hedging their bets in true British fashion. They see the American view is possible but tend to the view that it could be a clean sweep both for Presidency and parliament by the Movement for Multi-Party Democracy. They are beginning to predict a victory for what is now the opposition. The Japanese, whom you will of course understand are setting themselves up to be major players, not only in South Africa, but in the region as a whole (and if you are worried about their investment patterns in South Africa, then you need to look at their investment patterns in the region where they want to achieve economic dominance). They would like Kaunda to stay in power, but because they are very careful, pragmatic, they are hedging their bets with a fair degree of contact - with both the ruling government party and the opposition party. I feel the Japanese would like to see Kaunda remain as President, because they have a very good working relationship with him, but at the same time, the Japanese know that if investments are going to mean anything in the future, then there has to be a technocratic structure running the essential ministries in government , otherwise their investment patterns just aren't going to work. They would probably favour a split, as the Americans foresee, with Kaunda as President and the Opposition in control of Parliament.

What do I think are the prospects for October 1991? - the prospect is certainly somewhat enigmatic. The constitutional base in terms of which this is meant to be happening is still in the process of being argued. The actual date for the elections still hasn't been called and Kaunda will probably want to call that at the last possible moment, although he has promised October and I think that he will be in a great deal of political difficulty if he tries to postpone it much further. It will probably be in October, after the Commonwealth Summit in Harare, because one suspects that he has in mind one last triumphal entrance at probably his last Commonwealth Summit before disappearing into the political wilderness. With that comment, I think I have made clear my own prognosis: he is going to lose and by a significant margin. The Americans and British are both wrong in thinking that it is going to be a close run affair. My own opinion is that it is going to be quite a decisive defeat - but this is based only on my own intuitive appreciation of the politics of that country. There is no way to conduct a public opinion poll in Zambia. Although on paper it would be legal, it is politically unable to be accomplished. There would be so much trouble with ruling party vigilantes if you tried to do it. My views are gleaned entirely from informal soundings taken among not only the educated Zambians but also in frequent travels into the rural areas and into township areas and also from soundings from within the armed services as well, who have their own contingency plans. One way or the other I don't think that by this time next year President Kaunda will be able to call himself President any more, except very much as a courtesy retirement title. I must repeat: there is no formal evidence for this crystal ball gazing but as I said right at the outset of this talk, if there is a change of government and if the MMD people do come into power, then I would see a significant and immediate overture towards this country for economic liberalization in terms of trading links. This is not going to please the other Front-line states, who have in their own minds a fear that after a political settlement of one sort or another in this country - and although it may look rather distant now, most sane people contemplate an eventual settlement - there is the fear amongst the Front-line States that military destabilization will be followed by an era in which there is a

South African led- economic hegemony of the region. What they fear is that they will then owe everything economically to a financial and economic engine driven by this country, which will effectively overwhelm the economic structures of the Front-line States.

The reason why Namibia, and particularly Angola, are important to the Front-line States is because they see them in the long term as alternative economic poles to South Africa. While they are contemplating this vague possibility projected for a date in the future, their last wish, in the short term, is to see their allies and fellow-members deserting piece-meal to the enemy, as it were. If Zambia changes government, if its technocrats and businessmen take over and immediately start making trading and financial overtures to this country, this would be seen stepping out of line from what is at present a rather sketchy Front-line economic platform. Consequently there is unlikely to be too much enthusiasm among the Front-line States over the likely outcome of the 1991 Zambian elections.

CHAPTER THREE

DEMOCRACY IN SOUTHERN AFRICA: THE 1990 ELECTIONS IN ZIMBABWE AND 1991 ELECTIONS IN ZAMBIA (1992)

(with the assistance of Chanda L. J. Chingambo)

The eastern European revolutions of 1989 were watched with amazement around the world. Even in third world countries, aware that the superpower conflict was passing away, and with it what little international leverage they had, the scenes from the streets of Warsaw, Prague, Berlin through to Bucharest were captivating. In African countries it meant, for government machineries, that internal security systems would no longer benefit from East German and Czech inputs. For their educated elites, the rhetoric of leaders like Vaclav Haval, living in truth and being on the side of history, made sufficient use of a left wing vocabulary to blur the underlying prospect of an international victory for liberalism.

Not all citizen-driven protest for democracy is successful. China and Burma provide examples of brutal suppression. On the face of it, Africa seemed hardly a fertile ground for such protest. And not all movement towards democracy is citizen-driven. In southern Africa, the mid-1990s might see every state in the region, with the exceptions of Malawi and the kingdoms of Lesotho and Swaziland, governed under democratic constitutions, with multiparty parliaments. There will be varying levels of justiciability in the region's bills of rights, but the majority of presidencies are likely to be limited in tenure. Grand old men, like Kaunda in office from 1964 to 1991, should become anachronisms rather than the rule. Governmental change should be guaranteed, even if structural change is slow. This vision is being delivered piecemeal, however, and very differently from country to country in southern Africa.

In Angola and Mozambique, the painfully slow negotiations seek to provide not only a stable transition to democracy but a carefully managed one. There will be guaranteed room for both the MPLA and UNITA in Angola; and for both FRELIMO and RENAMO in Mozambique; the negotiators being aware that unacceptable losses for one of the major actors in the conflict could mean the postponement of peace. Outside powers such as the US, all the way to the Vatican, alongside regional powers such a Zimbabwe, anxious for a regional stability born of predictability, are playing their roles in the management of change - in the managed introduction of democracy.

In South Africa, democracy is not so much growing out of the principle of majority rule as subjected to the negotiated conditions under which majority rule might be possible. The National Party's platform of entrenching minority rights and privileges, while diluting as far as possible majority power, suggests the possibility not so much of managed change as the conditioning of change itself.

Multiparty states exist in Botswana and Namibia, the first having survived from independence achieved peacefully in 1996, and the second having been derived from an extraordinary spirit of cooperation in a constituent assembly born of armed struggle, superpower mediation, UN involvement, and a negotiating round of ten formal meetings from which what is now the SWAPO government was excluded.

In 1990, the government of Zimbabwe drew back from the introduction of a one-party state. In 1991, the people of Zambia voted out of office the UNIP party that had monopolized the years of the one-party state from 1973-1990. In these two countries that had made critical contributions to the liberation struggles of southern Africa - liberation being the precondition for democracy - the multiparty state had been secured in very different ways. In Zimbabwe, an elite in smoke-filled rooms had been as effective as the voting citizens; but, in Zambia, it was indeed a citizen-driven movement for democracy. This article looks at the background to multiparty democracy in both countries.

A word should first, however, be said about the animus behind the movements towards democracy in Zimbabwe and Zambia. Despite the captivation with what happened in eastern Europe, and despite public reference to the achievement of democracy there, eastern Europe has been more a metaphor than a model. In fact, the challenge to the democrats had been very much laid down by African leaderships who, in the case of Zambia, insisted that the 'scourge of multi-partyism', Kenneth Kaunda's words, could only wreak havoc by providing the window of opportunity long sought by barely-repressed tribalisms. In Zambia, the democrats sought to demonstrate that this was not the case.

In Zimbabwe, more pragmatic and personal issues were also involved. A one-party state would have reduced the scope for the leadership ambitions of several people, ostensibly well located within the governing ZANU/ZAPU coalition. There were genuine electoral misgivings about political society in Zimbabwe: the "Willowgate" scandal, over improper ministerial dealing in new cars, severely dented public confidence in politicians; but there is no evidence of major public disenchantment with the status quo. That adherence to the status quo, however, also meant a lack of public enthusiasm for its change in the direction of a one-party state. There was finally external opinion. This was to do less with western thought and more with changing thought on the African continent itself. On the eve of Zimbabwean party debate on the issue, at then end of June and beginning of July 1990, Julius Nyerere suggested that the one-party state could not be an indefinite institution in Africa and that the time was ripe for it to face challenge. [1] This gentle but deliberate removal of blessing from Nyerere was rumoured, in Zimbabwean political circles, to have been personally depressing for Mugabe.

Finally, again with Zambia, there was a felt need for change, even if it meant a plunge into unfamiliar waters. The risk of something unknown was balanced by a certain knowledge: Zambia was performing so poorly in economic and

[1] *THE HERALD* (Harare), June 29 (1990).

developmental terms that multi-partyism couldn't possibly produce anything less than the single party.

THE 1990 ELECTIONS IN ZIMBABWE

Zimbabwe was granted independence as a multi-party democracy; but, ten years after independence, as entrenched clauses in the Lancaster House constitution expired, the great debate was on the merits and, particularly, the indigenous nature of one-party rule. This would be rule in keeping with African 'tradition' and, to continue the generalised rationale, African needs. It would also be rule chosen by an independent African state, not imposed by the British as the Lancaster House constitution was seen to be. In the rhetoric of it all, it would be an act of constitutional freedom to reject the imposed political freedoms that accompanied independence.

Such a rhetorical context for debate in Zimbabwe never rose above manoeuvres within party politics that were driven by personality and pragmatism as much as grand general principle.

In the 1990 elections much attention was fixed on the ability of Edgar Tekere's ZUM to campaign and the results it achieved. These predicated discussion on electoral intimidation on the one hand and vote-rigging on the other. To concentrate on this very visible contest, however, is to miss two other areas of non-public intrigue and competition. Firstly, throughout the second half of 1989, the Harare rumour mills were working overtime on Tekere's attempts to forge a coalition between ZUM and dissident groups within both Mugabe's ZANU (PF) and Nkomo's ZAPU - by then joined together in their own coalition. The rumours suggested that highly-placed persons in Mugabe's Government, such as Edison Zvogbo, felt dissatisfactions; and, before the elections, Domiso Dubengwa, felt by many to be Nkomo's heir-apparent, made a public statement against the one-party state. A rebel coalition led by Tekere, Zvogbo and Dubengwa, the rumour mills suggested, could challenge successfully the Mugabe/Nkomo axis. As it turned out, both Zvogbo and Dubengwa campaigned vigorously for the government and, whatever their private feelings might have been, the establishment of a workable and credible rebel coalition would have taken time.

In the context of the 1990 elections, talk of such coalition could only have been fanciful.

Secondly and more importantly, there is the tension that continues to exist within Nkomo's ZAPU about the long-term viability and wisdom of coalition with Mugabe. As long as Nkomo remains leader, the 'meeting of minds' with Mugabe should stay unaltered. But he himself is tired and, eventually, must retire in favour of a younger man. It was he, rather than Mugabe, who extended his hand for the sake of coalition and unity, he who sacrificed the more and made the nobler gesture. Whatever Nkomo's history of opportunism, and despite the early history of dislike between Nkomo and Mugabe, he has now put himself comprehensively in favour of a united Zimbabwe. There is nothing more his career can hold for him. Yet, the succession is unclear. He still exercises a great patriarchal influence and, to complicate matters, Dubengwa does not have solid support within ZAPU. To outsiders, and particularly to western diplomats responsible for political reporting, he has appeared the logical successor, but there has never been any ZAPU consensus on this matter.

There is, however, the present author found, a remarkable underground consensus within ZAPU that the coalition with Mugabe might not last. There are two reasons for this. The first is the memory of the mid-1980s, when the 5th Brigade terrorised the Matabelelands in search of dissidents. This brigade of North Korean-trained thugs, who collapsed as a unit when faced later with a real enemy in Mozambique, left a lasting impression within the ZAPU base of support. Allied to this, many ZAPU politicians were harassed and incarcerated after the 1985 elections and, despite the surface charm of association with ZANU (PF), this has not been forgotten. The unofficial ZANU (PF) line is, of course, that ZAPU cannot have it both ways: their personnel cannot feel martyrs when , in fact, there was solid evidence of unlawful dissidence. Despite these arguments, the second reason is persuasive. Having entered a coalition, the ZAPU election message to its constituencies was that the election was one, not to enter parliamentary opposition as in 1985, but to share governmental power. That, after the 1990 elections, Mugabe awarded only three cabinet posts to ZAPU representatives was a great disappointment, and certainly rankled.

All of this cannot escape the shadow of what happens after Nkomo. Although there was a dispute over delimitation of his constituency - there had been confusing boundary changes - only 24.6% of the registered voters turned out in Nkomo's Lobengula electorate. Nkomo defeated his ZUM challenger 8,706 votes to 1,706, but many felt that his own constituents had delivered a protest note to the old man about his marriage to Mugabe.

Even so, it should not be assumed that ZAPU entered the elections alongside ZANU (PF) without any conditions. They laid down a very important condition, as will be seen below.

ZUM AND THE 1990 ELECTIONS

Faced with the combined might of ZANU (PF) and ZAPU, faced also with what can only be described as a campaign of localised vigilante intimidation of its candidates and supporters, culminating in the shooting of Patrick Kombayi, and faced lastly by its own organisational ineptitude, it is surprising that ZUM did so well. If a very rough parallel can be drawn, ZUM came to occupy - in terms of electorate support - the same position that the SDP-Liberal Alliance once held in Britain. This is in terms of votes gained, not seats won, and the achievement is not insignificant.

There are 150 seats in Zimbabwean Parliament. Of these, 120 are elective. Of these, ZUM won two, the party of the self-exiled politician, Sithole, one, and the government took everything else. In the presidential race, Mugabe defeated Tekere 2,026,976 votes to 413,840. The results of the presidential election were not made available constituency by constituency, but those from the parliamentary election were, and the present author has made a preliminary statistical analysis of constituencies around the four major urban areas of Harare, Bulawayo, Mutare and Gweru.

1. When calculated as the government has done, on the basis of legitimate votes cast, the percentage vote to the government appears larger than would be suggested by a cautious analysis.

2. When calculated on the basis of all votes cast, including spoilt ballots, the government share, while still sizable, is not quite as impressive.

3. There were a very great number of spoilt ballots and exactly what constitutes a spoilt ballot might be opened to question. In this, the third election since 1980, one might have supposed greater voter knowledge of how to fill a voting slip. This supposition cannot always be sustained, however, in the face of rural and even sizable urban illiteracy and poor education. It would appear that, in addition to ballots spoilt by incorrect voting procedure, correctly filled-in ballots were also disallowed if they contained additional comments - such as protest slogans. There is no way, except by anecdotal evidence, to suppose the number of 'protest' ballots. Many, faced with a choice between the parties of Mugabe and Tekere would not have brought themselves to vote for either.

4. Having said this, there is no sustainable evidence to suggest that the number of spoilt ballots was significantly greater than those of the 1985 and 1980 elections. Despite boundary changes, some patterns can still be traced and, on a nationwide basis, the present author does not feel that the 'deliberately spoilt' or 'protest' ballot scenario detracts from the impressive size of the ZANU (PF) victory.

5. Again, having said this, there were occasions in Manicaland when spoilt ballots, and how they were counted, could have materially altered if not overturned the final result. Manicaland was also the setting for some of the worst pre-election violence and intimidation. In public relations terms, it would have been better for ZANU (PF) if ZUM had won something like ten seats. The result could still have been portrayed as an overwhelming victory in western terms while suggesting fair play accorded an unpopular opposition. However, the number of seats where ZUM votes and all spoilt votes added together would have unseated a ZANU (PF) candidate still do not reach ten. So, even if localised rigging or miscounting can be demonstrated, and it has not been demonstrated - ZUM did not enter a legal challenge over any single result - it could not have significantly damaged the scale of the ZANU (PF) victory. There is no evidence at all of nationally-coordinated rigging.

6. The present author heard anecdotal evidence of irregularities in the counting of postal ballots, and some amusing anecdotes about minor irregularities in some polling stations, but he does not feel these could have materially altered the nationwide results.

7. The interesting factor was how few people voted, despite the election being extended to a third day of polling. By official register figures, 54% of the electorate cast votes - although the register is probably wrong and the percentage could have been higher. If there was an element of protest in absenteeism, some element - not to be exaggerated - of protest in the spoilt ballots, then these together with the ZUM vote and the votes accorded smaller parties suggest that, despite a huge ZANU (PF) victory in terms of seats, there is a significant though minor interest in favour of political pluralism.[2]

---

[2] For Zimbabwean reactions to the election result see, inter alia, Hasu H. Patel, 'The March 1990 Elections: Some Comment's *SOUTHERN AFRICA POLITICAL & ECONOMIC MONTHLY*, Vol.3 No 6 (1990); Hasu Patel, 'Political system shows successes, tensions and traumas', *THE FINANCIAL GAZETTE* (Harare), April 12 (1990); Donald Chimanikire, 'Zimbabwe Elections Reviewed', *SOUTHERN AFRICAN POLITICAL & ECONOMIC MONTHLY*, Vol.3 No.8 (1990).

ZUM did sufficiently well to remain the focus of political hope for a very sizable number of intellectual and professional people. Since the election, many professional groups have been on strike: teachers, nurses, junior doctors. Youth unemployment is growing drastically and the recruitment grounds for election vigilantes, the high – density townships around the main cities, are the unemployment catchment areas. Moreover, the vigilantes have seen how the party and government abandoned them when some were dragged before the courts on counts of election-related violence. The professional employed and those unemployed form a volatile electorate. ZUM's support can only come from such urban constituencies. The rural areas, while still not enjoying land reform and redistribution, are also the areas of worst education. The government's rhetoric, precisely because of its simplistic appeal, should continue to win the day there. Even in the urban townships, however, the ZNU (PF) apparatus is powerful. The local party leaders are deferred to and take precedence in the use of community facilities.

The real opposition base is among the intellectuals and, here, it receives a strangely reasoned support. The students who view ZUM as a left-wing alternative to the government are not really important in the Zimbabwean context. They have no programme, have a student administration itself accused of corruption, and allow stridency and shrillness to usurp the place of reasoned and principled opposition. This makes it all the more alarming and, indeed, stupid that the government should have closed the university in 1989. The non-student intellectuals include university staff members and civil servants, and this is why the government in 1990 issued fliers suggesting that all civil servants should be members of the ruling party. Some intellectuals certainly see the issue in terms of a preference for liberal democracy, but some see an historical necessity for a multi-party state - in the sense that 'every developing state, including every African state, must go through a period of liberal bourgeois government'. This is the old 'socialism is reached by stages' argument, and certain stages cannot be jumped. What they hope to achieve in a multi-party system, however, is quite radical, so that despite being labelled by the government as being on the right they in fact view themselves as very much to its left. The government is correct in fearing the opinion of intellectuals, particularly those in its civil service Zimbabwe has the best educated civil service in Africa. This means, enviably, Zimbabwe has a technocratic structure. It can be, as it was in Zambia, rendered meaningless by uneducated ministers and party officials, and any attempt to purge the civil service on party lines would mean the beginning of taking that risk.

ZAPU AND THE FUTURE OF PLURALISM IN ZIMBABWE

The MPs from the Matabelelands had extracted a promise from Mugabe at the December 1989 congress of ZANU (PF), that the one-party state should not be raised as an election issue. Throughout the 1990 election, although the issue lurked very much in the background, ZANU (PF) did not campaign on the basis that there would be a one-party state. When, after the elections, Mugabe claimed a mandate for a one-party state, there was dismay in ZAPU. This laid the foundations for an organized lobby within the coalition.

While the author was visiting Zimbabwe in 1990, the ZANU (PF)/ZAPU coalition Central Committee met on 29 June. This was the same day Nyerere was reported as coming out against the one-party state's perpetuity. And, in the preceding week, the government-controlled press published articles calling into question for the first time at length the viability of a one-party state.[3] The day after the Central Committee finished its business, the National Consultative Assembly met. This was composed of the separate central committees of both ZAPU and ZANU (PF) that existed before their coalition. This meant that, in a very short period, the central committees of both parties and of the coalition had met, and these formed the

[3] Charles Samupindi, 'One Party System has failed in Africa', *THE HERALD* (Harare), June 26 (1990); and Charles Samupindi, 'The One-Party State and Some Economic Effects', *THE HERALD*, June 27 (1990); although non-state media such as *THE FINANCIAL GAZETTE* and the church-owned *MOTO* (a courageous voice in the Smith years, which is why it cannot be suppressed now) have long questioned the desirability of a one-party state. The Catholic Commission for Peace and Justice emerged in 1990 as a major pro-democracy lobby.

most representative opinion possible within the ruling coalition. These bodies came out against the one-party state. Although this was not announced publicly, it would appear that, for the immediate future, Zimbabwe will remain politically plural with multi-parties permitted.

This will mean continued constitutional space for ZUM. It will also mean that if, in the future, dissidents from the ZAPU and ZANU (PF) wings of the coalition wish to splinter off, they can form a party, or more than one party, or unite to form the super-ZUM of Harare's visionary pundits. It will mean that, should it wish, ZAPU can become a party by itself again - although this is unlikely while Nkomo remains in office. It means, in short, pluralism and, within this pluralism, the ZAPU, ZANU (PF) dissident, and ZUM coalition scenario becomes extraordinarily attractive - because, if it works, it means a political force not based on tribal grounds, but cutting across them all. If this faces the government, itself a unified coalition across tribal groups in the 1995 elections, then even if it doesn't win (and it probably won't, given the government's showing in 1990 as discussed above), the spectre of determining tribalisms will have been proved mythical in Zimbabwe.

What of democracy in Zambia, however? This article will now recount the events of June and early July 1990, which laid the ground for multi-party pluralism.

THE JUNE 1990 UPRISING IN LUSAKA

The term 'uprising' is used, for this is what it was, not a series of riots. It began at Munali, on the eastern fringe of the city, when customers purchasing the staple maize meal were stoned by protesters who sought a boycott in reaction to its 120% rise in price. Munali is immediately adjacent to the university, where the students, almost by tradition opponents of Kaunda and his UNIP party, joined the protest. From there, it spread to the neighbouring township suburbs of Mutendere and Kalingalinga, the latter being itself adjacent to the mass media complex and the radio station. The three townships of Munali, Mutendere and Kalinglinga, together with the grounds of the mass media complex and the university campus, became the centre of the uprising. To the north of the city, the suburb of George rose up and, slightly to the south, residents of Kanyama joined in.

Ostensibly about the price of food, the uprising looted several supermarkets and most of the main street, Cairo Road. The government imposed a 24 hour curfew around Cairo Road, but reports suggest the police regarded it only as a dusk to dawn restriction. The breakdown in communications and command structure in the uniformed services that this suggested became graphically clear in the incident at the radio station where, by official accounts, a deranged signals lieutenant from the city of Kabwe single-handedly took over the station and broadcast for hours to the nation that Kaunda had fallen. It is impossible for one person to take over this radio station. It is part of a sprawling complex which is technically very sophisticated. One person could not have held the station, continued to broadcast, and technically kept himself on the air for any time at all. It is clear that a greater number of army personnel were involved and the firefight that ensued to retake the station left, according to unofficial reports, 19 dead. Other soldiers in the meantime cruised the streets of Mutendere and Kalingalinga, announcing the fall of Kaunda. There was some minor violence apart from the media complex and the death toll in total was probably higher than the 23 admitted.

Unable to rely upon his own army, Kaunda depended on his para-military force, his airforce, and detachments from old friends and neighbours. Again, according to unofficial accounts made to the present author, Tanzanian troops ringed the campus while the para-military rounded up the students and arrested their leaders - with customary para-military brutality. In a show of symbolic solidarity, according to these accounts, the Zimbabwean airforce flew in to bolster the position of the Zambian Air Commander - who was promptly appointed Minister of Defense.

The uprising was expressed in violence precisely because no other means sufficed. The rise in food prices, while real income dropped, contrasted sharply with the very visible wealth of party leaders. The statements reported in the treason trial of previous coup-plotters from the army, that Kaunda had himself amassed immodest sums in overseas accounts,[4] left him as the symbol of all that was wrong with the ruling elite and the ruling party. It was firstly inefficient and ineffectual. It was secondly dishonest and corrupt. It was thirdly self-perpetuating and irremovable. It, fourthly, received such advantages at the expense of the people. This became the agenda of protest.

KAUNDA AND RESPONSIBILITY FOR JUNE 1990

After the June uprising, Kaunda's remarks were vengeful. 'Those who live by the sword will die by the sword', he said, later adding that he might propose stronger penalties for coup plotters.[5] But the uprising had attracted international attention. British editorials judged that it was 'too late for him to save his reputation', and that his maladministration, vanity and economic incompetence could no longer be offset by the 'aura of statesmanship' which he had retained 'for an undeservedly long time.[6]'

Kaunda did try to save his reputation in July. On the international front, he secured the release of Daphne Parish from an Iraqi jail, where she had been held because of her friendship with Observer journalist Farzad Bazoft, who had been executed on spying charges. Even though Zambian officials insisted it was the culmination of a lengthy process, and not an overnight stunt designed to refurbish his image, Kaunda made the most of the occasion by having Mrs. Parish flown from Iraq to Lusaka, before sending her home to Britain, the roundabout route facilitating a press conference in which he could (and did) shine. Nationally, Kaunda released the prisoners taken in all three publicised coup attempts against him, that of 1980 involving Edward Shamwana, that of 1988 involving General Christon Tembo, and the most recent effort of 1990 in which Lieutenant Mwamba Luchembe had, in the

---

[4] *THE TIMES OF ZAMBIA* (Lusaka), 15 and 17 February (1990).

[5] *TIMES OF ZAMBIA*, 1 July 1990; and *DAILY MAIL* (Lusaka), 4 July 1990.

[6] *THE INDEPENDENT* (London), 29 June 1990.

official accounts, single-handedly taken over Lusaka radio to broadcast the advent of a coup. Blanket forgiveness had overcome his earlier bitterness.

The release of Daphne Parish was not without its idiosyncratic moments. Kaunda complained that the western media had been responsible for the death of Farzad Bazoft in Iraq. Media pressure on 'my brother', Saddam Hussein, had been so intense that Saddam, so as not to appear a pawn of the western press, had no choice but to have Bazoft executed. 'I have no doubt in my mind that, if it had not been for that vicious attack on him and on by Iraq by the British authorities and press, that man (Bazoft) might have lived, might have been here with Daphne together.'[7] Kaunda seemed to suggest that press attention on both Saddam and him had been willfully spiteful and wrong, and the intention of the press conference seemed to be an attempt to vindicate them both by parading a freed Daphne Parish. Whether this was the case or not, the choice of Saddam for a 'brother' could not have been more miscalculated as, the very next month, Saddam invaded Kuwait and precipitated not only immense international effort against him, but a concerted international recasting of his image. Yet Kaunda had not been caught in a trap of opportunism, naming Saddam as his 'brother' simply for the occasion of Mrs. Parish's release. Zambia had supported Iraq in its conflict with Iran, and Kaunda did indeed feel a close relationship with the Iraqi President, renaming the prettiest street in suburban Lusaka Saddam Hussein Boulevard. The problem is that, while it is perfectly possible to view Saddam as a champion of the third world, prepared to stand up against western domination of the world's interests, any such view can only be limited by Saddam's ruthlessness. It is perfectly possible that Kaunda misjudged the man, but such misjudgement would simply add to the confused list of his attributes that arose from the events of June and July 1990. In those two months he was a mediator, successfully negotiating Daphne Parish's release; a generous victor, forgiving his enemies who had sought to depose him; an object of dissatisfaction and blame from his own people and elements of his own army; an obstinate politician, monopolizing power, and refusing to abandon it in the face of vigorous protest and the declining abilities of his government to provide services; a declared admirer of Saddam Hussein; and, through it all, two months of crisis, he

[7] *THE GUARDIAN* (London and Manchester), 18 July 1990.

was a man of decisiveness. Whatever one's preferred judgment of Kaunda, he did not panic and took a series of calculated steps which allowed him to emerge scathed, but intact and still credibly the leader of Zambia.

The range of perceptions possible in that time, however, illustrates how difficult it is to pinpoint his personality. But, if Kaunda was decisive in an hour of crisis, then he was less so in the months leading up to it, toying with measures for constitutional change which could only have further centered power on himself and his UNIP party. In March 1990, 14 proposed changes to the constitution were gazetted, including one which provided that only the party president could be president of Zambia.[8] A week later, he told the UNIP Fifth National Convention that the changes in eastern Europe were only temporarily mesmerizing and that, in Zambia, the one-party state was there to stay.[9] In the beginning of April, however, parliament in a show of defiance failed to provide the two-thirds majority necessary to pass the second reading of the 14 proposals for constitutional change.[10] Prominent backbenchers, as had former UNIP luminaries at the Fifth National Convention, charged the government with a succession of failures, and the party with a hijacking of national power.[11] Clearly a mood of dissatisfaction was being expressed and, as a result, Kaunda promised to consider the backbench fears while on holiday.[12] In mid-May, Kaunda announced a referendum on a multi-party state, but spoke gravely against those who might seek such political pluralism, cautioning that it would be a recipe for tribalism.[13] Kaunda would himself lead the "no" campaign, denouncing the scourge of multi-partyism and, in this way, firmly staked himself to UNIP's record and the style at least of his own future on the referendum's outcome. It all seemed suddenly desperate and certainly stuff born

---

[8] *DAILY MAIL* (Lusaka), 8 March 1990.

[9] *TIMES OF ZAMBIA*, 16 Match 1990.

[10] *DAILY MAIL,* (Lusaka), 5 April 1990.

[11] For the full text of one such speech, see Sikota Wina, 'An Open Letter to the Fifth Zambia National Convention', *Southern Africa Political & Economic Monthly*, Vol.3 No. 7, 1990.

[12] *TIMES OF ZAMBIA,* 11 April 1990.

[13] *TIMES OF ZAMBIA,* 14 May 1990 and 25 May 1990.

out of isolation. If Kaunda had been in touch with national feeling when playing with 14 constitutional amendments, he would never have had them introduced in the first place. Once he took surroundings of the political climate, he announced measures to safeguard his position by firstly placing it under threat. None of this was adroit and, as it turned out, it was not particularly convincing. In June, the riots came and Kaunda's tenure was threatened with violence.

In the wake of the riots and his successful crisis management, Kaunda postponed the referendum from October 1990 to August 1991. Even so, an opposition movement began to flower that included several former UNIP figures. Released detainees, who had been charged with coup-plotting, did not rule out their participation in the opposition, and UNIP itself began debating radical changes to the party's powers and the longevity of tenure of the party president.[14] Finally, under mounting public pressure, of the sort associated with the pro-democracy movements in eastern Europe, but largely untracked by television cameras in Africa, Kaunda abandoned the idea of a referendum and instead announced multi-party elections for October 1991. The short-term history of this entire episode, from the introduction of 14 proposals to strengthen the UNIP grip on power in March, to debate on a radical loosening of this grip in August, to the September decision to allow a multi-party election, saw Kaunda having to move with a tide he had not anticipated. If, in crisis situations, he is decisive, then he can show less clarity of thought in longer-term political projections.

KAUNDA AND THE ELECTIONS

Kaunda made the announcement about multi-party elections on 24 September 1990, at the opening of the 25th UNIP National Council. It was an extraordinary speech, beginning with prayer, silence to mourn the passing of various UNIP luminaries, a note on the uprisings in eastern Europe, a defense of UNIP achievements and the value of Humanism, and a reference to the Zambian uprising of June. Then he

[14] *TIMES OF ZAMBIA* , 8-11 August 1990.

went onto deride the irresponsibility of the multi-party advocates. 'I believe too that as a developing nation we cannot afford the luxury of political debate for its own sake which will only delay development.' The introduction of such debate by the multi-partyists was 'not addressing itself to the core issue of the referendum', would only encourage 'divisions in the nation that can end up in bloodshed', and was seeking to win over 'the poorest of the poor in our society who have become target group of the Multi-party Party advocates."[15]

Using this reasoning, Kaunda announced that he was abandoning the referendum and going straight into multi-party elections. He said that UNIP would 'win any General Election against any other party.'

> Let us make these people who are now hiding behind empty multi-party slogans, who are shielding behind false accusations of oppression by UNIP sit down and think what it is like to run a real political party...Let us take them on comrades. Personally, I am more than ready to lead UNIP in an election against any party or parties in this country ...(I) recommend to you that we do not carry on with the referendum which was an excellent idea if everybody was prepared to behave in a civilised fashion but which has now been turned into an instrument for creating anarchy in the nation by some individuals and organisations not known for their democratic values, principles and practices. [16]

Although this caught the UNIP Council by surprise - Kaunda had not consulted UNIP on the elections issue - Kaunda at least had come out fighting, and sought to carry the fight to his opponents. The remainder of his speech was devoted to the revitalisation and democratisation of UNIP itself. In the early days of the year-long election campaign, however, UNIP did not behave in the most civilised of

---

[15]Address by His Excellency the President Comrade Dr Kenneth David Kaunda at the opening of the 25th National Council of the United National Independence Party at Mulungushi International Conference Centre, September 24- 29 1990.

[16]Ibid.

manners. The largest daily, *The Times of Zambia*, was told by Kaunda to 'project the policies of UNIP', and the pages of the paper were 'no longer for everybody'. Kaunda banned all parastatal and government bodies from advertising in the independent, church-owned weekly, the *National Mirror*, which supported the multi-party movement. He said that UNIP would publish 'terms of reference' to govern the media, including broadcasting.[17] In the city of Ndola, the Senior Governor announced that 'no one will live in a council house, ride on UBZ buses or enter the market without a UNIP card'. And UNIP officials instructed the Lusaka Governor 'to make it practically impossible for non-UNIP supporters to live in their areas.'[18] Kaunda also reshuffled his cabinet, sacking one minister outright and sending two to the foreign service.[19] Harassment of multi-party figures began, with some emphasis on the opposition leader, Frederick Chiluba, who was charged with illegal assembly in October 1990,[20] and removed from the board of leading parastatal in November.[21] Although Kaunda had called for a new UNIP, 'totally eradicating the paternalism of the past',[22] and which had to 'develop a brand new approach to the electorate',[23] the Senior Governor of Ndola, continuing the theme of making life difficult for non-members of UNIP, said that it was 'time to revert to the old tactics.' If Kaunda spoke of divisiveness being engendered over a referendum on the multi-party issue, then the year-long countdown to actual multi-party elections seemed set to eclipse his own projections, with himself in the thick of things, in the centre of a crisis, laying about himself with swings and hooks.

---

[17] *TIMES OF ZAMBIA* , 1 & 2 November 1990.

[18] See *TIMES OF ZAMBIA* , 4,9,11 November 1990. A court injunction was later gained against the Governor of Ndola.

[19] *TIMES OF ZAMBIA* , 2 November 1990.

[20] *DAILY MAIL* (Lusaka), 18 October 1990.

[21] *TIMES OF ZAMBIA* , 2 November 1990.

[22] See his speech, f/n 15 above.

[23] Ibid.

The students responded with vitriolic satire that was peculiarly Zambian. Posters were pasted up depicting Kaunda with genitals growing from his head. Slightly more subtly, but its meaning not lost on passersby, an immaculately scrubbed dog was tethered in Cairo Road.[24] But the true scale of protest against Kaunda was seen in the street demonstrations. In late 1990, in the small city of Kabwe, 40,000 marched for a multi-party state; and, if the international television producers could ever have thought that Kabwe had the same resonance as Prague or Gdansk, then their crews would have filmed something no less amazing, the dusty African streets thronged with the desire for pluralism and democracy. But Kaunda gave himself a long time, twelve months, in which to campaign.

THE CAMPAIGN

The campaign had three main phases. The first concerned the newly organized MMD (Movement for Multi-party Democracy), as the main opposition party, under Frederick Chiluba, clawing back its access to the media and asserting its campaigning rights in a series of successful court actions. By mid-1991, the UNIP position seemed sufficiently eroded for signs of disquiet to appear within UNIP ranks. In July 1991, Kavindele launched a fruitless challenge for the leadership of UNIP. Although Kaunda retained the UNIP presidency, may felt Kavindele had been a stalking horse for more senior dissidents who, in the end, felt the UNIP electoral chances were best served by closing ranks behind Kaunda. But by mid-1991 Kaunda too was showing signs of siege. South African papers gave prominence to Zambia's international debt position and the parlous state of Zambia's special pleading before international donors and lenders.[25] One revealed that, in May, Kaunda had sent a letter to donors, on the lifting of subsidies demanded by the IMF, saying 'if he raised the maize price his United National

---

[24] The implication being that no matter how clean an image the president tries to present, he is still a 'dog'.

[25] *THE CITIZEN* (Johannesburg), 22 July 1991.

Independence Party could easily lose elections scheduled for October.'[26] By this stage, the international financial community had lost patience with Kaunda's government and this disenchantment was picked up sufficiently in UNIP circles for Kavindele's challenge to seem worthwhile. The second stage, therefore, saw UNIP draw a collective breath but, by then, some within it, though outside Kaunda's circle, had already begun to contemplate the possibility of electoral defeat.

The third phase covered the run-in to the election itself, held on the last day of October 1991. Tensions were high and the police felt constrained by mid-October to caution both Kaunda and MMD's Chiluba against inflammatory statements.[27] It must be said, however, that inflammatory statements on both sides had characterised the entire campaign. Surprisingly short on sustained violence it had, nevertheless, been an ungentlemanly affair. As the election hour approached, passions and fears were high. In the last month of campaigning, October 1991, four major areas of electoral "irregularity" were debated between the two major parties - if charge and countercharge could be called debating.

1. BALLOT IRREGULARITIES. The longstanding MMD fear was that, somehow, the ballots, once cast, might be added to, miscounted, or lost - that, in short, the count would be "fixed". To prevent this happening, the MMD sought monitored counting at each place of voting - even though such monitoring would have imposed significant logistical problems. Transporting ballot boxes to central counting locations, as happened in the end, raised in MMD minds the spectre of interference en route. As late as the day before the polling, the MMD was continuing to express its fears in this direction.[28]

The related MMD fear was that, wherever ballots were counted, some attempt, somewhere in the process, would be made to stuff the ballot boxes. Again, on the

---

[26] *THE STAR* (Johannesburg), 22 July 1991.

[27] *DAILY MAIL* (Lusaka), 14 October 1991.

[28] *TIMES OF ZAMBIA* , 30 October 1991.

very eve of the poll, much protest was made at the revelation that 40 books of ballot papers had gone missing from the printers.[29]

2. UNIP FEARS OF THE OBSERVER GROUPS. The election was to be widely observed and two major teams, one a Commonwealth Observer Group coordinated by the Commonwealth Secretariat, and the other, a larger and somewhat clumsier exercise led by a former US President Carter, were soon encamped at Lusaka's Pamodzi and Intercontinental Hotels respectively. These two foreign groups added to internal observer groups organized by Zambians themselves which had attracted grants from foreign embassies.

UNIP felt most concerned about the two foreign groups. The first full-page newspaper advertisement on this subject in October was muted and reasonable, though somewhat plaintiff in its dissemblement of injured pride, putting forward the point that Zambians could organise a decent election by themselves, and that the observer groups smacked of an implicit paternalism on the part of western powers.[30] The second full-page newspaper advertisement was altogether a different product, and was lodged just 5 days before polling. Under the subheading, 'Imperialist Strategy for Zambia', it charged that:

> most of the so-called Observer Groups are in actual fact not election monitors, their assignment is to facilitate the removal of the UNIP Government and replace it with a puppet one like had happened (sic) in many parts of the world.

Citing Nicaragua as an example of an election ostensibly monitored but in fact rigged by outside teams.[31] Whether UNIP had genuine fears of endogenous rigging, or whether the advertisement was just a copywriter indulging in unconsidered rhetoric, the advertisement brought an instant response of outrage

---

[29] Ibid.

[30] *DAILY MAIL* , 3 October 1991.

[31] *TIMES OF ZAMBIA,* 26 October 1991.

from the observers.[32] On the very eve of polling, Kaunda had firstly to disassociate himself from the advertisement,[33] and then apologise to the observers.[34]

3. THE NATIONALITY QUESTION. This began gaining momentum before October and, indeed, there has always been a slightly submerged Zambian chauvinism on the matter, with doubts having been raised from time to time about Kaunda's own parentage, Malawian according to his detractors and not genuinely Zambian. In the election, however, the question was asked by UNIP firstly of non-black MMD candidates. Guy Scott, a white farmer and former Oxford don, was accused of being British; while Dipak Patel was charged with being simultaneously British, Indian, and Zambian - the implication being that his Zambian status was merely a flag of convenience, while he travelled the world on other passports and, anyway, according to some cruder charges bordering on racism, there were no black MPs in India, so why should there be an Indian MP in Zambia? The MMD also took up the theme of nationality, seeking to label the UNIP party boss in Chipata a Malawian and, therefore, ineligible even to live in Zambia. These charges and countercharges continued into the last week of the election campaign, prompting at last a newspaper comment that the whole issue had gone far enough.[35]

4. THE QUESTION OF DIRTY TRICKS. In October, the MMD published a full-page newspaper advertisement setting out its list of UNIP dirty tricks. Some were more serious than others but they were mostly fears of misconduct, rather than demonstrated large-scale misconduct.[36] Tucked In at the end, and somewhat lost in the extensive list, was a genuine complaint. This was to do with the restriction of the franchise to those who had evidence, i.e. voters cards, of having

[32] *TIMES OF ZAMBIA,* 28 October 1991.

[33] *DAILY MAIL* , 30 October 1991.

[34] *TIMES OF ZAMBIA*, 30 October 1991.

[35] *TIMES OF ZAMBIA*, 26 October 1991

[36] *DAILY EXPRESS* (Lusaka), 5 October 1991.

participated in the last elections. Despite a twelve month campaign, the government had insisted it had been unable to extend the voting lists or carry out new or supplementary voter registration. This meant that young people, normally entitled to vote for the first time in 1991, were ineligible in these historic elections. The MMD would, thereby, be deprived of a substantial section of its support. Whether this was a dirty trick, or sheer incompetence, can be debated, but it did raise what should have been the largest issue of any election - effective disenfranchisement - and the MMD should have laid more stress upon it, singled it out, rather than adding it to a catalogue.

Other October fears included MMD concern over rumoured UNIP plans to intimidate the printers of three new independent (and MMD supporting) newspapers;[37] MMD fears that UNIP was stockpiling weapons in neighbouring countries for use in the event of MMD victory;[38] fears that UNIP was training a private army;[39] fears that UNIP might seek to distribute T-shirts and chitenge (wrap-dress) material in exchange for voter cards;[40] fears that the police planned to arrest large numbers on the Copperbelt, an MMD stronghold, to prevent MMD supporters from reaching the polling stations;[41] and fears, again on the very eve of the poll, that UNIP agents had been giving rural illiterates false instruction on how to fill in a ballot paper in order to generate spoilt ballots.[42]

Again much of this was fear felt in a highly-charged atmosphere, but serves to indicate just how much tension accompanied the election. It also serves to indicate a certain political maturity in Zambia - that such tension never spilled over into sustained violence. There was certainly localised violence. Clear efforts were

---

[37] Ibid.

[38] *TIMES OF ZAMBIA*, 14 October 1991.

[39] *TIMES OF ZAMBIA* 28 October 1991.

[40] *DAILY MAIL* , 15 October 1991.

[41] DAILY MAIL, 18 October 1991.

[42] DAILY MAIL, 30 October 1991

made physically to intimate MMD candidates in the UNIP stronghold of Chipata. Kingsley Chinkuli, a UNIP Government minister, driving by chance into an MMD crowd on the edge of Kanyama, escaped with a very battered vehicle indeed. An MMD candidate, campaigning with his wife in Mandevu, was set upon by 12 UNIP vigilantes and, seeking to flee, fell over; whereon his wife, a karate student, bestrode her husband and fought off all 12. But, by and large, candidates were able to campaign freely, if not always at their convenience. Kaunda was himself pelted, but never really endangered. The campaign was ungentlemanly, full of fears and tensions, and robust. The MMD felt it had a hill to climb, as indeed it did, organising itself from nothing to take on the incumbency of a government that had been monopolized by one party since 1973, and a president who had been in office since 1964. Both party and president made full use of their incumbency. In more trivial but symbolic ways the campaign can be remembered as a battle of hand-signals. The UNIP gesture was a V for victory; but the MMD gesture was an extended thumb and forefinger, like their printed logo, a clock at one o'clock, the first hour of the third republic whose time had come.

THE DEFEAT OF KAUNDA

At the Zambia elections of 31 October 1991, Kenneth Kaunda was comprehensively defeated in the presidential race. His UNIP party became a rump of its former self and, after the parliamentary poll, holds only one sixth of the seats in the House. Immediately after his swearing - in, Frederick Chiluba renounced the presidential title of 'Excellency', and stated that new currency notes would not bear his portrait. Thus ended the Kaunda era. He had been in office since independence in 1964, and had been head of a one-party state since 1973. All over Zambia, his portrait began disappearing from public offices, where it had been mandatorily displayed, and private offices, where it had been displayed out of political politeness or political caution.

In his televised concession speech at 10am on 2 November, however, Kaunda was at great pains to appear dignified, forceful and generous. He did not cry into his handkerchief, spoke briefly and to the point, indulged himself in his rhetorical habit of repeating sentences only mildly, made only one statement that could be interpreted as sour grapes, and generally appeared the statesman used to the swings and roundabouts of a democratic culture. Only when he left the television studio and came to his limousine did he betray his feelings. Personally detaching the presidential pennant from his car, he wept as he handed it to his driver, climbed in and moved away. Even if forced, the dignity was a reprise of the Kaunda of old, a Kaunda who had faded since Zimbabwean independence, becoming only the echo of what his early biographers saw in him.

This public image of departure will perhaps linger. The new MMD (Movement for Multi-party Democracy) government is at pains to respect the contribution to nation-building of the old Kaunda, and there are no plans to prosecute him for real or imagined misconduct in office - even if several dossiers may be prepared. The sense of a coming-of-age was palpable after the results and, on 2 November at least, there was no urge to rake over a by-gone era. The rains that had begun early in the season had cleared for the elections. People queued all over Zambia from 5.am on the day of voting. Bright sunshine accompanied the poll, and also Kaunda's drive away through the dusty streets. He himself escorted the new President Chiluba on a tour of State House. It was an extraordinarily peaceful poll and transfer of power.

The background to it all paints a different image. After widespread rioting and an attempted coup in 1990, Kaunda was forced into announcing multi-party elections; he gave himself and his party a year to recognise and represent themselves anew; the franchise was restricted to those who had held it at the last election four years ago, thus depriving Zambians who had just come of age the right to vote, and thus seeming to deprive the MMD of its youthful support at the juncture where it would be most required; and the habits of free campaigning seemed hardly natural at first, with the opposition MMD party having to fight court battles for media space and to deny ownership of various media being transferred from Kaunda's Government to his UNIP party. As late as mid-October, Kaunda was promising to be 'merciless' with MMD leaders after a UNIP victory, and UNIP officials often found it difficult to refrain from bullying tactics as they campaigned. Right up to the eve of the poll, some UNIP officials indulged a flamboyant style : in Chipata, one red-shirted party boss, wearing a holstered pistol and introducing himself as the Saddam Hussein of Zambia, was accused of burning the houses of MMD supporters, and was certainly not noted for subtle canvassing.

For Kaunda himself, the campaign was an ordeal mixed with more personal tribulations. His son, Kambarage, was tried on charges of murder and sentenced to death. Rumours abounded in Zambia that other members of his family might shortly be arraigned on murder charges. At the Commonwealth summit, Kaunda flew to Harare for the opening ceremony, then flew straight back to Lusaka - the first time he had excused himself from the full duration of the summit. On Zimbabwean television, he looked pale and drawn, although it must be said that here, as in his concession speech, he tried to act in a stately manner, ensuring his photo was taken alongside Britain's John Major, and smiling determinedly for the 1,000 journalists present.

The image of the peaceful transition of power is a true and necessary one. The citizen-driven movements for democracy in eastern Europe are now being paralleled under different conditions and for different reasons in Africa. Zambia became the first African state in which a single-party government left office because of the ballot box. Zambia has become an example. Right up to the announcement of results, however - results that seemed painfully slow in coming at first - reports abounded of cheating and rigging. The newly-founded *Daily Express*, an MMD-supporting paper, had the headline 'Poll Scandal' on its November 1 front page, with accounts of fake ballot papers having been discovered. The *Times of Zambia*, originally a pro-government and pro-UNIP paper, which had moved towards reasonable coverage of both major parties, had as its front page headline, 'Anomalies mar polling day', followed by stories of minor irregularities in different parts of the country. With the nation on tenderhooks, there was a distinct tension in the air at the end of a year-long and, although largely peaceful, bitter campaign. By

11 am on 1st November, however, sufficient results had been announced to indicate a landslide return for the MMD; and at 4pm that day, the Commonwealth Observer Group, monitoring the freeness and fairness of the elections, announced that:

> the results ... fully reflect the will of the Zambian people. The entire process had shown that there is a basis in Zambia for the development of multi-party democracy. There is no doubt that events on Election Day throughout the country will provide lessons for other countries which intend to change to a plural political system.'

But, by then, the tension had already disappeared. Drivers all over the cities of Zambia flashed the MMD hand signal from their windows, grinning and beating their cow horns. There seemed little other celebration - simply a resigned feeling of relief; relief because they had ended it all, ended the Kaunda and UNIP era; resignation because the times ahead will be hard for them.

The final results were indeed a landslide, making the projections of Zambian political scientists, published in another new newspaper, the *Weekly Post* (29-31 October 1991), seem cautious and modest. But that itself has been a benefit of the new pluralism. Newspapers have sprung up; political debate is open; contrary to a survey in 1989, when the present author found not a single shop devoted to the selling of books in the entire country, some modest bookshops have opened. These things are important to the continuation of pluralism. Important to the reinvigoration of development will be the abolition of the UNIP commissar structure, which provided a parallel administration across the country to everything the government did. Often the UNIP expenditure on itself in any one region was greater than the funds government agencies had for development programmes. The programme of liberalism on which the MMD stood is meant to open Zambia to foreign investment and encourage private enterprise in an economic culture which has been centered on inefficient and unimaginative government control or monopoly.

Whether foreign investors will come, or whether Zambian private business can properly function in a land of deteriorated infrastructure is another question.

More importantly, the MMD was only ever a consortium of disparate interests, united in an opposition to Kaunda. The new President Chiluba was a necessary but not popular choice for many MMD luminaries. The MMD is packed with disparate ambitions and may not be stable in office. Chiluba struggled to present his first Cabinet. If domestic politics look likely to become, over time, fractious, what will be the foreign policy of the new government. What will be the image and reality of its behaviour in southern Africa?

In broad international terms there remains the problem of Zambian debt. In per capita terms, Zambia is the world's most indebted nation, and honeymoon writing-off or writing-down of bilateral debts will not fundamentally alter commercial bank debt or IMF debt. The IMF might itself extend some grace period to Zambia, but this cannot reduce the fact that the nation's future, and future development, have been mortgaged. Foreign policy will have an economic flavour.

In the region, the new government cannot play Kaunda's former role. The historical image of patron of liberation may linger but the era of liberation groups needing Zambian support ended two years before Kaunda's hold on power also ended, with agreement over Namibia. The residual conflicts in southern Africa, in Angola and Mozambique, are being mediated by non-African powers - United States, Portugal, Italy and the Catholic church - with some Kenyan and particularly Zimbabwean negotiating advice having been directed towards Mozambican antagonists, but with neither country having been able to act as principal brokers. The MMD hierarchy has not, for the most part, enjoyed close contact with the principle ANC negotiators and advisors to Nelson Mandela. President Chiluba has, himself, little international relations experience, although he has made a favourable impact in conferences of the international labour and trades union movement.

Determination to leave the past behind and to choose a new, pragmatic path in foreign policy, unconstrained by the image of support for liberation, came swiftly.

The new government opened diplomatic relations with both South Africa and Israel. The recognition of South Africa opens the way, MMD strategists hope, for South African - led investment. For the energies of the MMD will be devoted to domestic change and revitalisation. For this, it will seek, as a principal regional policy, closer economic contacts with South Africa. This will mean that, unlike the attempt made by SADCC (the Southern African Development Coordination Conference), to strengthen horizontal or broadly-based transnational economic linkages in the region, Zambia will seek to strengthen the vertical linkage between itself and South Africa - bypassing the emphasis on developing linkages with others in what has been the frontline. The image of the frontline will itself fade from the region, and the change of government in Zambia - with the new Zambian preoccupations - will hasten this process.

Within the MMD, however, are several constitutional lawyers, some of whom are distinguished in the field of international human rights. The new Minister of Legal Affairs, Dr Roger Chongwe, was six years Chairperson of the Law Association of Zambia, was also President of the African Bar Association, and is President of the Commonwealth Lawyers Association, and is frequently consulted by organisations such as the International Commission of Jurists. The concerns of such individuals will continue to find a place in international fora and, because they are now government members, this suggests that the previous generalised concern of Kaunda on human rights issues will be replaced by a more detailed and sophisticated advocacy. In this field, as in its domestic programme, the MMD expects to bring to bear the weight of its technocratic wing.

Not all the claims of technocracy are credible, however. Some cabinet ministers are clearly recycled UNIP, politicians who required the rewards of office for having jumped early to the MMD. Some are suspected of dubious international business dealings. With this mixture, there is unlikely to be any MMD ideology or social philosophy. There will be no more Humanism, and no further appeals to a universalistic set of ideals. The new Zambia, the Third Republic, was accomplished by a citizen drive for pluralism. It is citizen-centred not, as in Kaunda's Humanism, "man - centered". It is concerned with constitutional rights, and not with the pastoral images of a cooperative kingdom. In Zambia, the hour has come for something beyond Kaunda. In southern Africa, and the mesh and mash of the foreign policies there, Kaunda and his images have slipped into history.

The slippage had both portentous and odd symbolisms. By November 1991, an enterprising Kitwe artist was marketing a calendar of his drawings, set in the Garden of Eden. On one page, rhinos and monkeys strum guitars in celebration of the MMD victory. On another, Chiluba joins the manger scene overlooking, with Joseph and Mary, the infant Christ; and, on a third, God's sword-bearing angels drive Kaunda from Eden.[43] The slippage into history, or the expulsion from Eden, was narrated on Zambian television's effort at a non-stop election results service. Early on 1st November, then throughout the day, the Vangelis theme from Chariots of Fire, played either on a harpsichord or demented electric piano, backgrounded the litany of UNIP losses and MMD gains. If this was indeed a foreign influence, it was a plangent one.

THE REGION AND PLURALISM

Although southern Africa will by the mid-1990s be a largely democratic region it will not be a region of co-equals. If nothing else, South Africa's economic shadow will loom over its neighbours. In what may be seen in hindsight of years to come as a prototype of investment, economic activity in Mozambique's Beira Corridor gives a display of international involvement in which the only regional actor is South Africa. In his visits to Zimbabwe over 1990 and 1991, the present author consistently asked for details of Zimbabwean investment plans, only to be told that none existed and that the Cabinet had not requested any to be prepared.

This does not mean a lack of what is now the frontline's influence on the future region. It does mean that, economically, this influence will not match South Africa's. Politically, however, the frontline has its activists. In the settlement of

---

[43] *TIMES OF ZAMBIA* , 13 November 1991.

conflict and mediation, though without major triumphs, Mugabe has been in recent years both more active and active in a more sustained fashion than Kaunda - who was given to spectacular gestures, such as his summit with President de Klerk in 1989. The extent of Zimbabwean mediation is only now beginning to be recorded.[44] What it means is that the political conditions for a peaceful, and then democratic, region owe something to influence beyond South Africa's. If, during the 1970s, Zambia and Kaunda were seen as the regional patrons of liberation, it may be that in the late 1990s Zimbabwe and Mugabe will be seen as patrons to the political state of the region with, in Angola and Mozambique, controlled pluralisms arising out of the war waged by South Africa.

With Zambia, however, willing to open its doors to South African investment in an essentially economic foreign policy; and with Zimbabwe more economically resilient and a little more independent; the regional futures of these two democratic countries, each of which achieved pluralism in very different ways, seem set to diverge.

[44] See Hasu Patel, 'Zimbabwean Mediation', in Stephen Chan and Vivienne Jabri (eds), *Mediation in Southern Africa*, London: Macmillan (forthcoming).

CHAPTER FOUR

DEMOCRATIC ZAMBIA: A MID-TERM REPORT (1994)

In 1990 and 91, the streets of Zambia were thronged with demonstrators for democracy and, increasingly, for the new MMD party. If the world's television cameras had found the dusty avenues of Kabwe as attractive as the ice-blown dockyards of Gdansk, then the spectacle of tens of thousands of marchers might have suggested that, as in Europe, old regimes were being overturned in Africa. The MMD invented a soundbite, 'the hour has come', and a hand-signal, thumb and finger held at one o'clock, one hour after midnight, time for the third republic and, if nothing else, at least the semiotics of change. By mid-1994, with two years to go before another set of elections, both the substance and the image of popular, transparent democracy have declined. Hopes have withered. Many years ago, a young and cloaked Colonel Ghaddafi would stalk the Tripoli streets at night to see for himself whether hospitals functioned and people had places to sleep. In 1994, President Chiluba of Zambia, without recourse to a cloak, prowls ministries at 8am and ticks off workers, even ministers, who are late; but such calculated populist gestures do nothing to disguise the fact that something central has gone awry in the new Zambia. It seems a long time back to the 1980s, when President Kaunda slighted the then-union leader Chiluba, by called him a physically 'little' man. Miners took to the streets, chanting 'six foot four out! four foot two in!' Now, Chiluba looks diminutive enough to seem out of his depth.

Unlike its later counterpart in Kenya, FORD, the MMD held together throughout the 1991 election campaign. Kaunda had hoped it would divide and the vote be split sufficiently for him to come through the middle, as Kenya's Moi in fact did. The MMD was a coalition of disparate interests, and disparate ambitions. Several of its heavyweights were former UNIP ministers who would have wanted to become president - hence Kaunda's hopes for a split - but all knew they could never succeed to Kaunda's throne as long as he retained power. Chiluba was a compromise candidate and the other ambitions, taking a long-term view, held firm around him.

Chiluba came to power without any governmental experience. In order once to neutralise, or at least better observe him, Kaunda had offered Chiluba a place on the Central Committee of his UNIP party, at that time in the mid-1980s akin to a politburo - but Chiluba had refused him. Chiluba thus came to power, untried, and indebted to the MMD barons, particularly those who had financed its, and his, election campaign.

Despite this, the first months of the new government seemed an era of belief. Ministries began to function in a more technocratically accomplished manner. Increased bilateral and multilateral liquidity flows were made available. The new ministers seemed genuinely interested in their portfolios and in doing an excellent job. Under the surface, however, some cynicism underscored the outer idealism. It was rumoured that, at the very first cabinet meeting, ministers agreed to turn a blind eye to (sometimes their own) Mandrax smuggling. A single suitcase of the pills, manufactured in India and transshipped to South Africa from Lusaka, could bring in a fortune to its dealer at R5 a pill in the Johannesburg nightclubs. Even so, it took the drought of 1992 to bring to the surface the practice of corruption that had also taken root. Then it became clear, though not proven, that various ministers and officials benefited from relief imports. When the agriculture minister, Dr Guy Scott, left office after having been, in the opinion of many observers, unjustly harassed, several other MMD luminaries began to consider their positions. What followed was a departure of several ministers from office. Some left the MMD entirely, and established the National Party which, thus far, has enjoyed mixed fortunes at by-elections, and has established only a minor strength, seemingly centered on the west of the country. Its foundation conference was an organisational disaster, with many delegates unprovided with lodgings or even sustenance. Other departing ministers remained within the fold of the MMD, but declaring unease and vowing to fight for change. Half way through 1994, the Vice President, Levy Mwanawasa, resigned office, taking out full page advertisements in the two daily newspapers, saying he was unable to play a meaningful role in government, and that the behaviour of some of his colleagues struck at 'the very roots of good governance and transparency.' He remains with the MMD, however, but seems set to join those who resigned before him, such as the highly-respected civil rights lawyer and former justice minister, Dr Rodger Chongwe.

In the same time period of June 1994, Chongwe was embroiled in a much-publicised controversy. Chiluba's son, Castro, had been arrested for wounding a young woman. Police investigating the case seemed to be showing little sign of progress, and Chongwe said that, if the authorities, including the president, were seeking to delay or influence enquiries, then the president should be impeached.

This may have been Chongwe the old civil rights campaigner simply making a watchdog's point; or it may have been a signal that the president is now a target of party reformers and that the battle for the heart and soul of the MMD has begun in earnest. Chiluba, meanwhile, is beholden to those powerful party barons and ministers who remained in office - so much so that he appears often merely to be the chairman and balancer of others' agendas, but is able to take a few initiatives of his own. Meanwhile corruption has risen apace and, unlike the Kaunda era, the new regime has seen consumption becoming steadily more conspicuous.

At the same time, living standards for most Zambians have declined drastically. Inflation runs at well over 100% and, although a good range of consumer goods and food is now available, only an economic elite can afford them. The informal sector, particularly petty marketing in such items as secondhand clothes, has mushroomed, while the formal sector has experienced difficulties with growth and liquidity.

Zambia, however, has stick consistently to the structural adjustment guidelines favoured by the Bretton Woods institutions, and continues to score performance points with the IMF and World Bank. Indeed, financial policy seems designed with them in mind, with the Zambian citizenry as a longer term client group. What this means is that the citizenry is disgruntled now, and will be in the middle term. More time, and greater liquidity flows will be required before Zambia can emulate that other darling of the IMF and World Bank, Ghana. In fact, to draw a superficial analogy, what Lusaka resembles in the mid-1990s is nothing so much as Accra in the mid-1980s. But Chiluba faces elections in 1996. What can he deliver to Zambians before then?

Chiluba has to deliver little for the plain reason that his opposition can only deliver less. The National Party does not differ greatly from the MMD in economic policy. Indeed, its leaders helped frame that policy. Many of its senior members, however, are tarred with the brush of having jumped twice, first from UNIP and now from the MMD. The public perception of them as inconstant opportunists has already begun to hang heavy, in addition to their poor organisation and isolated geographical support. The other opposition party, the rump of Kaunda's UNIP, should maintain its seats in eastern Zambia, but it is undergoing a root and branch structural overhaul and has basically decided to concede the 1996 elections with (some say futile) hopes of victory in 2001. 1996 will again be Chiluba's year, but voter participation may be conspicuous in its meagerness.

If Chiluba is true to election promises that any president should be limited to two terms, then 2001 should indeed mark a watershed in Zambian politics. It is with that year in mind that factions within the MMD have now begun jostling. Some veteran politicians would still like to be president, or to have become very rich if the presidency proves impossible. Some still feel the MMD, in its early idealistic form, remains a cause worth fighting for and the party redeemable. The opposition should be better organized by 2001, so that 1994, although mid-term in Chiluba's first term of office, is probably quarter term in his presidential career overall. There are a number of plus points to what has been accomplished in Zambia.

1. Chiluba has ended the personality cult of the president, disdaining the title of His Excellency and declining to stamp his portrait over banknotes; he has disdained also the acquisition of doctoral titles by way of honorary degrees, but has himself studied successfully for an MA of Warwick University.

2. To Chiluba's credit and sense of tolerance, there is an active and vocal independent press. Unlike its counterpart in Nigeria for instance, criticism of the government is usually researched and well-written, but seldom fails to carry a sting.

3. Some important symbolic measures have been taken. There is now water at the national University Teaching Hospital, basic medicines and anesthetics, and the wards are clean and the gardens tended.

Each of these points has its reverse decor, however:

a. Chiluba is a weak president, without long-term policy vision or long-term muscle to implement policy if it impinges upon the interests of a powerful minister.

b. The opposition press is essentially one bi-weekly newspaper, *The Post*, so if push came to shove it is only one paper that needs to be censored or shut down. This should not be necessary as the government still controls broadcasting, particularly the vernacular radio stations.

c. If the University Teaching Hospital has been symbolically refurbished, the University of Zambia has been run down and a lecturers' revolt crushed. Outside the University Teaching Hospital, rural health care is under-researched, with Zambian-trained doctors migrating overseas and their places filled, if at all, by foreign physicians, including Indians and Cubans.

Other demerit points concern foreign policy. The Zambian government seems to have lost considerable brownie points with the new ANC government of South Africa, and this is probably due entirely to maladroit diplomacy. Zambian peacekeepers are stationed in Mozambique and, while performing competently, are doing so against the odds, having been sent there without proper equipment or resources. Kaunda would have been a difficult act to follow in foreign policy but, as if determined not to be associated in any way with Kaunda's legacy, Chiluba's foreign profile is distinctly low, at times submerged.

It has all been a disappointment to those huge numbers of Zambians who walked the dusty streets in search of democracy and its fruits. Yet, that there will indeed still be multiparty elections in 1996 is a not inconsiderable accomplishment. This is an accomplishment of the citizens. The government they elected has few accomplishments to its credit, but will survive until 2001, by which stage structural adjustment may or may not have done its work. If it has, Chiluba will seek to claim credit. Under his presidency, perhaps under anybody's, Zambia is passing through a period of mortgage. Most Zambians seem to know that the third republic is a transition which must be endured.

CHAPTER FIVE

ZAMBIA AND THE DEMOCRATIC EXPERIMENT (1996)

The results of the 1991 elections in Zambia were unexpected. In a country without opinion polls, and under a one-party state (UNIP - United National Independence Party) since 1973, with a formidable one-party political structure down to ward level, opinion in the diplomatic community had guessed a return of Kaunda as president but for a MMD (Movement for Multi-party Democracy) challenge for parliamentary supremacy. That UNIP was reduced to an Eastern Province rump, and that Frederick Chiluba comprehensively defeated Kenneth Kaunda surprised almost all foreign observers. Locally, however, the groundswell for change had been highly visible. The rallies for multi-party democracy, attended by tens of thousands in dusty streets, were every bit as resonant with the romance of liberty as the rallies in the freezing shipyards of Gdansk or on the boulevards of velvet Prague - Kaunda gave the most dignified of concession speeches, personally removed the presidential penant from his car, and escorted the Chiluba's around State House before vacating it. It was a graciousness rare in African politics, and it contrasted with the rancour of the campaign, still more with the turmoil of Zambian policy-making as, over the preceding decade, Kaunda had slowly lost his grip and touch.

In 1996 Kaunda is seeking to run for president again. The early idealism of MMD lasted one year in office. In that time, foreign agencies and missions noted a genuine increase in governmental efficiency and technocratic input in policy formulation and project documents. Gradually, however, these positive features faded before the imprint of two key issues that concern the electorate in 1996.

1. Growing resentment at economic hardship, even while Zambia gains plaudits for its structural adjustment efforts from the World Bank and IMF, and succeeds in having many of its bilateral debts written down.

2. Increased crime and corruption among government leaders, ranging from Mandrax drug smuggling to extorting 'commissions' from international investment and other capital inflows.

In addition, there are two issues of political freedom that are less tangible but highly important in any democratic contest.

1. The attempted use of constitutional reform to bar Kaunda from contesting the elections, widely seen even by non-supporters of Kaunda as fixing the ground for Chiluba. Under moves to introduce a new constitution, Kaunda could be regarded as a non - Zambian citizen; the incredulity surrounding such a move only serves to reinforce the impression of a low ebb in the tides of Zambian political culture. There are other draft constitutional provisions that limit judicial independence and make for a Gaullist presidency of the type the MMD once campaigned against in Kaunda's reign.

2. The prosecution and imprisonment of newspaper editors from *The Post*, a paper which had pioneered press support for multi-party democracy championed the MMD and Chiluba - but then used exactly its earlier standards of democratic performance in appraising the new government, finding it and its president wanting.

Finally, there are three issues of political organisation which should make the 1996 elections volatile.

1. The MMD has never established the organisational structure of UNIP. Its ability to mobilise is less concrete and pervasive.

2. UNIP has retained, but only in part - no one can really gauge how large a part - its organisational structure but its cadres are well-known and able to be targeted in the event of a violent run-in to the elections. Moreover, UNIP briefly split and, although its alternative leader, Kebby Musokotwane, a former Prime Minister and Finance Minister, died, UNIP is not the power it was. There has been no patronage to sustain it as before. In addition, technocratic members, such as Kennedy Shepande, have deserted it for other parties.

3. The other parties that exist are small, have had tribal appeals that have nevertheless been short-lived; and/or are essentially elite vehicles. Highly able former cabinet ministers, such as Dr Roger Chongwe, an internationally - acclaimed human rights lawyer, who have founded parties have not discovered any common touch.

Whoever monopolizes vernacular radio time will have a competitive edge in rural areas. Whoever fields the most "muscle" - or party militants as they are known in Zambia - will have a competitive edge in the poorer urban and extensive peri-urban areas (Zambia's population is 70% urban or peri-urban). The level of political culture now being low, all parties being not as organized as they would wish, and with full fields of leaders and former leaders on all sides with mixed records of honesty or its lack, the campaign will be violent but not in the Natal mould. An appropriate analogy is hard to find - except perhaps with the distant example, in more highly developed form, of Mexico. Locally, it will be less violent than Natal, more violent than Zimbabwe in 1990. In short, it will be a flawed election with which the international community can live.

All serious parties, however, campaign on precisely the same economic platform. There is seen to be no choice but to accept World Bank and IMF programmes for economic recovery, despite their social costs. Given this, there may well be considerable abstention at the polls.

Who will win? Probably Chiluba and MMD, which makes their panic about Kaunda all the more curious. Kaunda and UNIP should, however, improve considerably over their 1991 performance, if only for nostalgic hankerings for his time when things were bad but not as bad as now. Zambia's is, however, a very sophisticated electorate, well versed (as is Zimbabwe's) in the debate over economic structural adjustment, and knows very well that today's economic problems were sown in Kaunda's time. UNIP should break out of its Eastern province stronghold and make modest but visible gains in larger urban areas. Other parties may pick up single figure seats in the west and south but should not be a meaningful fixture in the body politic. What does this mean for the region? Outside of South Africa, Mugabe of Zimbabwe will remain the dominant political figure and Zimbabwe will continue as the only other reasonably developed if embattled economy. Zambia will not be a desirable state for South African investment, both because of corruption and lack of infrastructural reliability. It will, however, be a market for World Bank contract work, such as highway and other transport engineering, as Zambia reaps the rewards of observing World Bank and IMF conditionalities.

Having said all that, Zambia retains a regional role. Its peacekeeping troops - demonstrating that Kaunda's philosophies of peace were more than merely facile - are deployed in force with UN missions. They were present in Mozambique and Rwanda, and are present in Angola. They are seriously underequipped but surprisingly professional despite this, and their presence points a finger at Zimbabwean and South African peacekeeping postures.

Chiluba is not a statesman. A chairman among his MMD barons, many feel he has been out of his depth. Conscious of his lack of education and fretful when compared with bookish Kaunda, he has devoted long hours to extramural studies with the University of Warwick gaining an MA and now reportedly working on a PhD. Since, however, Kaunda's reputation survived longest in the international arena, Chiluba has been very hesitant to venture into arenas where comparisons might be harsh. Foreign and regional policies are formulated or guided by others, some of whom are suspected of using the region for purposes of international crime. It is not, in whole or part, a salubrious or promising foreign policy profile for a state once highly respected for its international activism. Mandela and Mugabe now share Kaunda's old crown of regional patriarch. As for Kaunda, now in his 70s, the 1996 elections have to be his last hurrah. Invested with a new lease of life, some see him as impressive as the Kaunda of the 1970s, but mortality attends even the most resurgent of men. For Zambia then, there awaits another five years of dissatisfactions in which, despite all, a painfully slow economic recovery might just start reaching the bulk of the population. It will also be a time when the MMD will war within itself to find Chiluba's successor in 2001, unless of course the reformed constitution allows third terms, and provided Chilubas Zambian citizenship is not seriously challenged.

FURTHER READING

- Douglas Anglin, *Zambian Crisis Behaviour*, Montreal: McGill - Queen's University Press, 1994

- Stephen Chan, *Kaunda and Southern Africa*, London: I. B. Tauris, 1992

- Frederick Chiluba, *Democracy in Zambia*, Lusaka: Africa Press Trust, 1993

- Kuaku Osei-Hwedie & Muna Ndulo (eds.), *Issues in Zambian Development*, Boston : Omenana, 1985

- Stephen Chan, '*Democracy in Southern Africa : the 1990 elections in Zimbabwe and 1991 elections in Zambia*: The Round Table, 322, 1992

CHAPTER SIX

TROUBLED PLURALISMS: PONDERING AN INDONESIAN MOMENT IN ZIMBABWE AND ZAMBIA (1999)

This paper is based largely on extensive interviews, conducted in both Zimbabwe and Zambia, with political, diplomatic, dissident and military personnel, who have asked to remain unidentified. Largely anecdotal, all anecdotes reported here have however been sustained in an elaborate system of cross-referencing the interview materials. In addition, the author held extensive discussions with citizens from the poorer quarters of Harare and Lusaka, as well as businessmen, journalists and academics. The author is thankful for a research grant from The Nottingham Trent University.

PROLOGUE

In May 1998, citizens of Indonesia took to the streets to defy the Government of President Suharto. The extent and depth of national anger shocked the political elite into a dramatic recasting of the cards they had habitually played for three decades, and Suharto was persuaded to retire. Although the same elite is still in power, Suharto and his family are no longer able to treat Indonesia as a private patrimony. What the citizens accomplished may, in the long term, seem very little. But the energy in their moment of intense effort to accomplish something *amorphously called "change" and, particularly, to set a limit to corruption, stirred beleaguered citizens in faraway lands, as they contemplated those whom they had elected to serve their nation ransacking instead its meagre reserves. The point of explosion, when mass patience snaps, is the Indonesian moment" of a brief African, surprisingly public, discourse.*

INTRODUCTION

COULD ZIMBABWE BECOME INDONESIA ? That was the question on the lips of those from the poor suburbs of Mbare and Mabvuku to the diplomatic diners on the capital city cocktail circuit in Harare. The events of May 1998 in Jakata may have been a set of transitory images in southern Africa; but citizens of Harare remembered their own riots in January of that year, in which large-scale looting took place and President Mugabe's name was regularly excoriated. Months later, the resentments still festered but, always a city of the most exotic political rumours, Harare festered and speculated - the essential difference between Suharto and Mugabe, who had been friends, is that Mugabe's Zimbabwe still permits a sometimes harassed, usually circumspect, but remarkable freedom of expression - but did not riot in the streets. On the campus and in the trade unions, most of May was a month of adjusting to the so-called wintry chills of high-plateau Africa and, while the citizens buried their concerns under their own warm jackets, sun-bathing tourists would have found little to suggest anything abnormal. The British pound and US dollar bought more than ever before. Therein, however, lay part of the problem; for the Zimbabwean dollar now bought even less than before and, all over Zimbabwe, eyes turned to the northern neighbour, Zambia, and people wondered whether it was now Zimbabwe's turn to slide as Zambia had financially slid.

Prophetically, as the Zambians had initiated their own food riots in 1990, which led eventually to the electoral fall of Kaunda, Harare's principle newspaper editorialized that 'the riots naturally gave rise to fears that something similar could happen here,' before dismissing the possibility;[1] although, during the 1992 Zimbabwean drought, the tune changed. "Remember how we all laughed at those Zambian riots? How we thought it amusing that people could take to the streets to toyi-toyi about the price of food? We ought, as the saying goes, to be laughing on the other side of our faces."[2]

In May 1998, Lusaka, the capital of Zambia, prepared for the treason trials of 82 people allegedly involved in the abortive coup of 28 October 1997. This resulted, among other things, in the government of Frederick Chiluba placing Kenneth Kaunda under house arrest (his house was subsequently gazetted as a prison); holding an opposition party leader, Dean Mung'omba, in appalling prison conditions, where he contracted TB and where, persistent rumours insist, he has been regularly beaten; and driving another opposition leader, Dr Rodger Chongwe, probably the finest legal mind in Africa, into Australian exile.[3]

Lusaka is small. Within the elite, friendships and hatreds are intimate. Sometimes Zambia seemed not a state at all, but a gigantic parish, where both good and (increasingly) bad behaviour was tolerated within a politesse that must be credited, at least in part, to Kaunda's exceptional blend of paternalism, patronage, barely-disguised authoritarianism, and ethnic balancing.[4] To the citizens of Zambia what had now broken down was not only the economy, but that politesse, Kaunda's unwritten but well-understood 'social contract' with the people - in which the elite cooperated and savage reprisals, while always held in reserve, were uncommon and applied to specific individuals rather than generally. There was an important extension of that politesse: the elite were rich, in large part corrupt, but the conspicuousness of consumption was limited; there was a decorum about dishonesty; that has now disappeared, and many ministers are wealthy in a style that invites comparison with their counterparts in Kenya. Thus, while Zimbabweans wonder if they will be the next Zambia, Zambians look over their shoulders at the spectre of Kenya, with its gross corruptions, crime rate, ethnic murders, and fractious politicians full of self-aggrandisement and vanities.

What follows in this preliminary paper - the full research document is forthcoming - is an account of the author's visit to Zimbabwe and Zambia in May 1998, itself an extension of the years he lived in those two countries and his regular visits since 1980. It ponders a snapshot and, above all, seeks to clarify the rumours and vocabulary of rumours that are used in political discourse in the two capitals. It then takes its own part in this discourse by speculating about the future. More than almost anywhere else in the author's experience, Zimbabwean and Zambian people and politicians invent or imagine futures. That so few come about is both a tragedy for ordinary people and their hopes, and their major blessing - for some politicians' dreams have nothing to do with the people at all.

ZIMBABWE

In 1992, deft and adroit political management by Mugabe, and some not inconsiderable statesmanship, even in the wake of the death of his wife, Sally, bought him great domestic acclaim for ensuring no one starved during that year's drought; and great international acclaim for his role in the Rome peace settlement between the antagonists in Mozambique. These were the last acts of Mugabe as a significant leader. In part, his handling of the 1992 drought merely postponed the growth of disenchantment with his ZANU (PF) party. Six years later, his party is unpopular and, beneath the surface, riven into at least three factions; and he, himself, remarried to a much younger and rather less popular woman than Sally, is a shadow of his former self, and seems at 74 to be unable to grasp the great pressures now moving upon Zimbabwe. Perhaps he should never have contested the 1995 elections - which he and ZANU (PF), in coalition with Joshua Nkomo, won very convincingly indeed. But he was still popular from 1992, although ZANU (PF) was less so; and the elections seemed to bestow upon him a renewed mandate. He could certainly claim so. Long-mooted, but not yet achieved, constitutional changes, however, propose a shift in presidential terms to provide for parliamentary elections in 2000, but presidential ones in 2002; ostensibly and quite reasonably to ensure continuity in the event of significant electoral change. But, with 2000 approaching, and with no opposition party able to challenge ZANU (PF); and with 2002 four years off, with no official successor to Mugabe in sight, and with the "old man" growing older in his ideas by the year, sudden drops in the value of the national currency, and sudden rises in the price of food, engendered a sudden sense of despair and helplessness. Elections would not help against the only organized show in town, and presidential elections seemed far off; as prices rose and incomes fell, high-level corruption seemed to grow. Against the backdrop of rival factions within ZANU (PF) playing games of political advantage over proposed constitutional changes, strikes and rioting broke out from 19-21 January 1998.

But, if ZANU (PF) was the "only organized show in town", how really organized is it in the middle of 1998? And, were the riots as disorganised as they seemed? These are the key subjects of rumour in the Harare mills. Starting firstly with ZANU (PF), it should be said that its coalition partner, Joshua Nkomo's ZAPU, may itself shortly be facing change. Joshua Nkomo is old and known to be ill, and prepared to facilitate a transition to new leadership. In that case, the favoured successor will be either John Nkomo or Dumiso Dabengwa; probably Dabengwa because of his greater appearance of gravitas and his popularity among the Ndebele people. Essentially, however, this means that there are at least four factions within the ruling coalition: one group not as easily predictable as the previous ZAPU, and three, if not more, groups within ZANU (PF), not counting popularist mavericks such as Margaret Dongo - who has attracted international attention as a rare female (and brave) politician, but who has little powerbase outside her own constituency in Harare. (Although expelled from ZANU (PF), Dongo remains a quintessential ZANU (PF) - style politician, and is regarded as a dissident ZANU (PF) politician rather than a dissident politician without any affiliation at all.)

One faction congregates around Edison Zvogbo, easily up to now the most powerful and audacious claimant to the throne, someone whom even Mugabe circumnavigates rather than confronts head-on. Zvogbo returns that favour and respect, and has not challenged Mugabe directly, staking only a claim to Mugabe's succession. He has been doing this for years now, holding high ministerial and party office all the while. A man of considerable (caustic) wit and taste, he has been ever a deliberate and cautious player. Deemed to be behind recent injections of radical proposals into the constitutional debate, such as the limitation of two terms for any one president, others have absorbed the counter attacks for him, and Mugabe's own wrath was directed against the speaker of Parliament, carefully omitting Zvogbo himself. The problem with Zvogbo could well be that he waited too long. Still capable of audacious movement - he recently made a personal apology to the Ndebele people for the atrocities of the Fifth Brigade in the Matabelelands in the mid-1980s, thus distancing himself from responsibility within a Mugabe Government, and signalling a desire to 'cooperate' with any successor to Nkomo - he has however fallen ill. The rumour mills suggest ravages of alcohol, but there is no evidence of this. What it does mean is that a loose ethnic coalition within ZANU (PF), which forms a not insignificant part of his powerbase, the Karangas of the south-east/south-central, and the Manicas of the east, may well lose their rallying point and organized animation.

These two groups feel particularly disadvantaged precisely because they have felt increasingly excluded from the levers of power and administration by Mugabe and his loosely-designated Zezuru people - and particularly so with the advent of his new wife, Grace. If the succession goes to a member of Robert and Grace's ethnic group, ZANU (PF) may split along ethnic lines.

Attempting to combat this is a grouping loosely known as ZANU (PF) Reform. Animated by Dr Ibbo Mandaza (who, unless he accomplishes a 'Jerry Rawlings', i.e. compensates for a half-European parentage, will never himself be president), this is the technocratic, youthful and intellectual wing of the party. A considerable intellectual in his own right, Mandaza operates a large publishing empire, including a long line of books on African democracy, and the recently launched *Mirror* newspaper. Someone who has personally felt Mugabe's wrath, he nevertheless seems to retain some respect for the president. His concern seems to be to revitalise, reunify and reform the party; and to revitalise it as a technocratically engaged and modern organisation.

Whether, in a still largely rural country, this has any resonance outside Harare is a question in point. Even more to the point has been Morgan Tsvangirai's fiery criticism of Zimbabwean intellectuals of precisely Mandaza's ilk:

> Zimbabwe has the misfortune of producing so-called progressive intellectuals who have the habit of lecturing workers and peasants through journals published from their mansions in low-density suburbs.[5]

Having made this criticism, it should also be made clear that Tsvangirai is himself an intellectual. As such, and as the leader of the Zimbabwe Congress of Trade Unions (ZCTU), he not only heads a 'fifth force', outside ZANU (PF), but makes of himself a clear distinction with Zambia's President Frederick Chiluba, who also was a national union leader, but has none of Tsvangirai's intellectual weight, despite endless effort in extramural graduate studies, while Zambian President, with Warwick University. There is, thus, some ruefulness in the jokes about border meetings between Zimbabweans and Zambians, in which the latter offer to trade Chiluba for Tsvangirai with the former. The thing about Tsvangirai, however, is not whether he is an intellectual or makes a good joking comparison with Chiluba; it is that many believe he and the ZCTU were behind the January strikes and riots. If there is to be an Indonesia in Zimbabwe, therefore, it will be led by Tsvangirai; just as Chiluba headed Zambia's Indonesian moment of popular unrest, leading to change in 1991. Mugabe cannot touch Tsvangirai as long as he heads the ZCTU, but Tsvangirai has no party machine, no popularity in the rural areas, and no experience in government. His attack on intellectuals like Mandaza was at least partly unfair. Neither running a publishing house nor being a trade union boss will win the rural vote. There is no viable opposition party. All ZANU (PF) has to do is to stay together. The size of voting absenteeism, particularly in the rural areas, or the return of a greater handful of non-ZANU (PF) MPs, particularly in the urban areas, will be what intensifies the inner-party battles, and it may be this that leads a triumphant delegation of barons to Mugabe's door to insist he not stand in 2002.

What is the code that represents all this? No one, despite considerable freedom to do so, publishes such a list of five forces within Zimbabwe itself. Certainly no one writes of Karangas and Manicas against Zezurus. There is here a politesse, uniformly guarded by all concerned. The country is one country, even when it is not. In short, a mythology sustains, and sustains very well, the concept of Zimbabwe. However, the unwritten talk of tribalisms should only partly be taken in a literal sense. It is, in some other part, as with Zvogbo's overture to the Ndebeles, to do with powerplays. That is easily enough understood. But it is also a code to do with concern about corruption. If, hypothetically, Mugabe secures the succession for another Zezuru, would this be because he feels the need for one of his own to protect not only himself in his retirement, but his rumoured, though hypothetical 'ill-gotten gains'? People talk of a South African - style Truth and Reconciliation Commission, but, even without the threat of prosecution, the prospects of humiliation may be cloaked in the protective veil of tribal language.

It is, of course, also that code which answers the rational thrust of Western analyses and Western prescriptions. It posits one rationality as a resistance to another. This should not necessarily be taken beyond its point of opportunism and excuse-making. However, it is a 'rationality' which is not only an 'imagination', but one that is couched in metaphor. There is at work here a discourse which proceeds by a mixture of actualities and metaphors, and the analysis of Zimbabwean politics needs to distinguish one from the other; and to interpret sometimes one in terms of the other. This is not necessarily new. It was implicit in the debate among Ranger, Lan, and Kriger, about magical beliefs and the actual bloodiness of warfare.[6] It is, however, to say that 2000, and particularly 2002, need to be seen not so much in terms of western images of democracy (there will be no challenge between equals at the polls; no other grouping will rival even a barely coherent ZANU (PF)), but to be seen in terms of international images, such as those of Indonesia (and against the background of Zimbabwean street power in January 1998), and in terms of national images of power-broking, betrayals and realignments; the declaration of both moral and technocratic high grounds; and the real as well as metaphorical uses of ethnicity in a struggle both for power, and not to be disadvantaged if out of power.

Who will be President of Zimbabwe in 2002? Probably not Mugabe or Zvogbo. The first will not recover his popularity and will continue to reveal his age. The second may be very sick or not be alive. None of the old guard, and none of the new young technocrats. The moment of the technocrats may come in 2012, two terms after 2002. Not Margaret Dongo or any other temporary darling of the

Western press. Not Dabengwa : for all the talk of metaphors, the Shona majority probably would still find an Ndebele president hard (but not necessarily impossible) to swallow. Tsvangirai? He's tested his street muscle. Simultaneously, he is reinventing himself as a highly reasonable (but implicitly aspirational) African version of Tony Blair. His spin-doctoring, or use of political language is Premier League stuff. Tsvangirai on the January riots :

> You have to be very discreet when you are dealing with a government which has fascist tendencies. Our role is in the workplace and we are still developing the social movement in this country. But I will say that when a government takes decisions, such as deploying soldiers, that does affect people in the workplace, and it is intolerable.[7]

However, from the street, through the uses of language; from the cities to the countryside; from the intellectual (but not doctrinaire intellectual) to the brutal uses of politics; from no party to defeating a great if divided party; to the corridors of State House will require something like an Indonesian moment. The offspring of Zvogbo, the hard men of manoeuvres and deals, will rally to the party. And, if they select a hard man to succeed Mugabe, the authoritarian drift of the government will continue. In Zimbabwe, the Indonesian movement may not come till 2006, one year before the end of the first term of a new authoritarian president; or, if he, against all odds, hangs on, one year before the end of the fifth term of Robert Mugabe, then 82, the ghost of Hastings Banda in a land where so many fought to receive, at century's end, so very little, and where they and their children rose briefly in the streets one teargassed - filled January.

ZAMBIA

In May 1998, at the Lusaka Theatre Club, near the three great hotels of Lusaka, its Cathedral, its Supreme Court - both stone lions now restored after Rhodesian commandos delighted in blowing one of them up - and its major Ministries, playwright Maurice Tembo's satire, 'Does the President Know?' was staged. Of course the implication was that the president knows everything, but does nothing, as his ministers run amok, chasing their own advantage and lining their own pockets, forgetting the days of 1990 when, in dusty streets throughout the hugely urbanised country, an Indonesian movement seized Zambia, and the citizens forced democracy upon the state and changed its government. The audience laughed at every barely disguised reference to well-known politicians and the structure of their peccadilloes; a bitter enough laugh as, once, though 1990 seemed an historical epoch ago, the self-same politicians were idealists at least of sorts and, Lusaka, indeed Zambia, being small in its elite, each member of the audience probably remembered a friend of sorts, once gulping beer as his dinner guest, chastising loudly the Kaunda Government, but now removed to a ministry of his own - perhaps eyeing the presidency itself in 2001, when Chiluba will have exhausted his constitutional two terms - and sipping imported brandies in a world of a faraway morality. Bitter too as each theatre-goer well knew, as the country knows, the emotional energy of an Indonesian moment - because, briefly, many people, with very little, risk everything - cannot be repeated for many years to come. Chiluba's MMD party is the only real show in town, and no satirist can write it out of the script.

Indeed, the suspicion is that elements, at least, within MMD have been seeking to write others out of the script; and, in response perhaps, elements within the army have considered - some actually tried - the wherewithals of a coup and the restoration of honesty and transparency, since democracy of an electoral sort (even though the government had decimated the opposition) was still, in a procedural sense, available. This part of the paper ponders events in Zambia from August 1997 to May 1998. In May, 82 people were about to stand trial for a coup attempt in October 1997. Much is now *sub judice*, so the material presented here is circumspect, while narrating stories somewhat different to official versions or even 'widely-known' versions.

August 1997

On 24 August 1997, Dr Kenneth Kaunda was still free and, in loose coalition with fellow opposition-party leader, Dr Rodger Chongwe, was addressing an illegal political rally in Kabwe. Police opened fire, ostensibly shooting into the air to disperse the crowd.

The format of the Kaunda/Chongwe rallies had become standard. Kaunda would introduce the national anthem, sit down after it, and Chongwe, never the great orator Kaunda clearly was, would address the crowd in clear, slow, complex but thoroughly explained terms. Suddenly there was a politician who did not patronise his audience with simulations of rhetoric. Kaunda, whose role was to answer questions afterwards, knew well the public mood to do with IMF and World Bank structural adjustment packages, economic liberalisation, and legal issues to do with the extent of the president's powers and his constitutional mandate. This is a far more sophisticated electorate than many thought and Kaunda, finally, though it had to drive him from office before he believed it, now believed it; and he let Chongwe pick holes in the MMD like a courtroom barrister would pick holes in a learned counsel's stupid case. No orator, Chongwe; but sardonic, almost foppish - he had to be persuaded not to campaign in his cream suit and panama - he now disciplined his eccentricities to devour the rationalisations of the MMD Government.

It was not the roadshow most had expected. Many, as a result, came to view it all as Kaunda's subtle attempt to woo Chongwe, and other opposition leaders, into a grand alliance which would, effectively, be a Greater UNIP - based on the organisational core of his own UNIP party, but with the appearance of a technocratic government-of-national-unity in waiting. More than that, some saw it as Kaunda's finally recognising that he, himself, was no longer electable, both because of history and Chiluba's constitutional tinkering, and that, no great untainted talent being available within UNIP proper, he was annointing Chongwe as his successor. It was an amazing scenario but, on the stage in Kabwe, an internationally-acclaimed lawyer was giving his political speech when the police opened fire.

Chongwe and Kaunda fled to their car. Here, the official story is that a loose or ricocheting police round accidentally hit the car, passed through the back window frame, grazed Kaunda's head, and passed through Chongwe's neck.

The UNIP account having first claimed to have recovered the spent shell of the bullet responsible, and having claimed to have had it forensically examined in London, is that it was an assassin's bullet, deliberately aimed, by good fortune misguided, and that it carried an explosive charge.

This does not really hold up since, if it was an explosive bullet, it should have exploded when it hit the car's window frame. Moreover, it begs the question as to whether the intended victim was Kaunda or Chongwe. It would take a very ambitious assassin, of cinematic skill, to attempt targets, through a metal frame, with one shot.

At first, Chongwe's car set off on a mad dash to Lusaka. It became clear, however, that he was loosing too much blood to reach the capital. The car swung around, cinematically indeed eluded the pursuing police, and reached Kabwe Hospital where, by good fortune, a former army surgeon, experienced in trauma, saved his life. The bullet had entered through his cheek and had, miraculously, missed all major nerves, arteries and bones, before smashing its way out of the back of his neck. It was very messy, but he lived.

A few days later, recovering in his home, his neck swollen to twice its normal size, Chongwe was receiving well-wishers. One was Dr Guy Scott, leader of yet another small opposition party, and once a great friend of Chongwe. A renowned atheist, Scott's first words were, 'My God, Rodger, its a miracle you're alive!' To which, the weak but droll Chongwe replied, 'Ah Guy, don't tell me that in your late age you have finally acquired faith.' When style greets the bullet, there is something to be said for persevering with the study of Zambian politics.

One intelligence source, however, privately speculates that there were two bullets. In short, Kaunda and Chongwe were both targets. The bullet that came through the back window frame was intended for Kaunda. The frame distorted its trajectory and it hit the car ceiling and, its force being largely spend by two interim impacts, its ricochet grazed off Kaunda's head without severity. The second bullet was discharged as Chongwe, attempting to find fresher air than the teargas that had swept in to the car, put his head through the side window. The bullet meant for Kaunda was incompetently discharged, but the one meant for Chongwe rather more expertly so.

What does this mean? Has assassination really come to Zambian politics? It is hard to believe that any official plot would have been enacted so publicly. To an extent, this is now the sort of fertile ground for conspiracy theories like those still emanating from Dallas. But the nameless intelligence source is impeccable so, perhaps, someone, somewhere, in some part of the official apparatus, made a unilateral decision. Or, perhaps, it really was clumsy and misdirected police fire. It is hard, however, to fire into the air and hit two separate occupants of one car not yet moving on the ground. Perhaps one, or two, police officers acted in the heat of the moment and took pot shots at the opposition car. There is no evidence to sustain any account. The result, however, was palpable enough.

October 1997

On 28 October 1997, in the early morning, a doomed coup attempt rolled out of the Lusaka barracks in armoured cars that boasted few rounds of ammunition (the gunnery quarter-master was not in on the plot), and with one strategic objective. That was to capture the army commander, General Nobby Simbeye, and force him to announce over national civilian radio and television that a coup had taken place, and to order, over the army communications network, adherence to the coup.

The latter part of the objective was probably wise. Presidential loyalists in the Kabwe garrison would otherwise have counterattacked, led probably by the deputy army commander - an adherent to a strict separation between civil and military spheres - and it was the Kabwe garrison that had the tanks, ageing TR42s, but stout enough to withstand even endless rounds of fire from the ordinance on armoured cars - before rolling over them. Probably about six TR42s could reliably have been expected to reach Lusaka. If that makes the coup attempt, and its possible response, something like a Gilbert and Sullivan musical, the unfolding tragicomedy would have its full share of tragedy as well.

Recognising the engine whine of the armoured cars from afar, Simbeye fled on foot from his home. Finding him gone, the irate soldiers broke into his liquor cabinet, drunkenly raped his wife, then even more drunkenly set about their main business by steering a route to the president's State House. One day, a scholar will fully analyse that destabilising link between idealism and the bravado that allows someone to march to overthrow the state; and the grievance and hurt, from poverty and deprivations, especially relative deprivations - as felt by the rank-and-file soldiers as they entered the general's luxurious home - that drives someone to loot and rape, and be unable to pass up a moment's full luxury, even while on business to point guns at a corrupt, but electorally legitimate government.[8]

Outside State House the soldiers demanded the president's surrender. Inside, Chiluba was probably ruing the day when, in order to score a cheap and unnecessary point, he had shown on national television the network of tunnels under State House, which he claimed had been used by Kaunda as torture chambers. But they also provided escape routes from State House, and he had shown those on television as well. Now, he probably imagined soldiers outside and beneath, ready to explode at any minute into the banqueting hall which, years before independence, had been designed to look like its counterpart at Buckingham Palace. What Chiluba didn't know was that the rebels had little ammunition and, even though they were simultaneously taking control of the suburban Chelston barracks, and the national radio studios, and the small inner-city airstrip one mile from State House, Simbeye was rallying loyalist forces and, by 8 a.m., the night's adventure had ended and the putsch crushed. Its alleged field leaders, Captains Stephen Lungu and Jack Chiti were arrested, and the hunt began for its animators in the political sphere.

Dean Mung'omba, an opposition party leader who had actually contested the 1996 presidential elections against Chiluba, was arrested and what can only be called a brutal incarceration began. Kaunda, who had been constitutionally prevented from contesting those elections, was out of the country but returned. The government waited before arresting him, in an amazing show of neglect for public relations, on Christmas Day 1997. Caught on camera, the arresting officer was apologetic to the point of deference to his prisoner. Whoever advises Chiluba on these matters might benefit from a crash course in situational presentation. Kaunda was transferred to house arrest on New Year's Eve, but Mung'omba languished in jail. Questioned on television as to why Mung'omba could not enjoy the same comfortable captivity as Kaunda, Chiluba point-blank replied that the international community seemed not to care as much about the one as the other. Indeed, Julius Nyerere, along with the USA, Britain and South Africa, had all asked for Kaunda's proper treatment. The same grouping, including a personal appeal from President Mandela, had petitioned Chiluba to allow Kaunda to stand in the 1996 elections, but had been refused. The similar appeal from Commonwealth Secretary-General, Emeka Anyaoku, had been greeted almost with disdain - Anyaoku having been given vague assurances during his visit to Zambia, only to have the government reassert its course as soon as he had returned to London. Many Lusaka-based and international commentators agreed with the view of the *Economist*, which described Chiluba's 'dogged efforts to exclude the former president (as) crude and personal.'[9] And they extended that judgement to Chiluba's treatment of Mung'omba.

Dr Rodger Chongwe, also out of the country was charged *in absentia*. Here the story becomes a moment of dramatic tension and indecision, before a last minute decision. Determined to return to Zambia to vindicate himself, Chongwe was taking his seat aboard a British Airways flight from Harare to Lusaka. Again overplaying its hand when it should merely have waited, the Zambian Government dispatched its own special plane from Lusaka to Harare to 'invite' Chongwe home with the president's compliments. British Airways refused to allow the Zambian agents aboard the BA flight. Zimbabwe aviation officials also refused. They referred the matter to Mugabe's private office. Whatever one thinks of Mugabe, he can see international embarrassment better than his Zambian counterpart. The prospective headlines, 'Zambian agents drag opposition leader from British Airways flight at Harare Airport', not to mention a basic respect for aviation laws and normal procedures, had Mugabe's office order the Zambian agents back to Lusaka. Meanwhile, the BA flight, delayed and waiting on the tarmac, was preparing at last to leave for Lusaka. Chongwe was pacing up and down the aisle. A stewardess brought a fax to him, then the airplane steps were removed and the doors were about to be closed. Chongwe finally made up his mind. He went to a stewardess - by now the entire staff knew that here was a man choosing between escape and a probably brutal imprisonment - and the steps were brought back. Chongwe left the plane and boarded a flight for Perth, where he had been a student and married an Australian national, and from where he now looks over the Indian Ocean towards Africa, wondering if he ever might return. The last-minute fax had been from his family in Lusaka, begging him not to return, informing him the climate was murderous, and Chongwe, a hole healing in the back of his head, finally realised discretion might be the better part of valour.

Chongwe is not the only politician to have fled in exile. Others, for instance in Cape Town, are the subject of detailed rumours. One of the last senior politicians actually arrested was Princess Nakatindi Wina, related to the alleged coup Captain, Jack Chiti, by marriage. The two had been seen meeting before the coup. Of them all now, a discreet silence is in order, since court proceedings have begun.

What the government itself may not know, however - or is not making public - is that there were almost certainly not one, but two, and even possibly three coup plots being simultaneously hatched, each ignorant of the others. The botched coup was the one led by the most junior plotters and, although they had a national agenda of sorts, chiefly aimed against corruption, they had also an army agenda. Men had not been paid, allowances had been removed, yet certain very senior officers seemed richer than any pay structure could suggest. The second coup plot was almost a classic late-twentieth century reprise of the sociology of Nigerian coups in the 1980s: young and technocratic Majors and Colonels, with a national agenda (which may or may not be corrupted after a taste of power), which in this case called for an interim cabinet of national unity, and fresh elections within six months, without any restrictions on the right to stand of the sort Chiluba had introduced.

What had saved Chiluba had been the launch, before the others, of the most inept of the plots. Lusaka buzzes with talk of an army major, who died mysteriously in a car accident - conveniently, even if with the mordant Lusaka wit attached to the stories - outside the Ambassador Funeral Parlour, one week before the coup attempt. To which of the coups he was affiliated, and supposedly a principal animator, is unknown; if to the second coup plot, then his death probably delayed its execution; in its place, a motley crew of lightly-armed, drunk soldiers, NCOs, and two Captains set out to displace Chiluba and, in the process, probably saved him. The government has been more alert since and, as Zambians wryly note, has been trying a little harder to be a government, rather than a club of millionaires.

If this is true, the difficulty of the prosecution case resides in which of these plots, if any, senior defendants were involved, or about which they were merely informed. For the government can gain political advantage from having overcome an inept coup attempt. If it knows about, or admits, the existence of a far more sophisticated plot, suggesting unrest is wider and its own position more precarious, then it admits to a substantial unpopularity. If the prosecution does not identify the existence of other plots, for which no military officers have been arrested - the government can also know discretion before valour - then if may have great difficulty linking sophisticated and experienced politicians to something of the tragi-comic simplicity of 28 October. But, if the politicians are released by the court, Mung'omba will emerge from prison a physically broken man. In a narrow game of points, the government is ahead.

The Games of the Future

On June 1 1998, what will be a protracted and complex treason trial opened in Lusaka. Heavyweight lawyers, including former Prime Minister, Daniel Lisulo, and star academic, Professor Patrick Mvunga, appeared in the defence ranks. Dramatically, Kaunda was released. White-bearded now, Mandela had brokered a deal by which charges were dropped 'for lack of evidence'. Finally seeking to redress some international image, Chiluba acceded - for once - to the region's elder statesman. Having said that, the story of Mandela's access here is itself astounding. Mandela cannot stand Chiluba, thinking him unstatesmanlike. Chiluba, on the other hand, cannot bear being held in such low regard by such a great man. Since Mandela's earlier appeals to Chiluba to allow Kaunda to compete in the elections had fallen on deaf ears, Mandela this time asked to travel to Zambia as a private citizen, to visit Kaunda in his prison home. He made it clear he would not travel as a president, and did not want to meet Chiluba. This was clearly the most calculated of diplomatic slights, even an insult. This was too much for the prickly and proud Chiluba to endure, so, finally, he allowed himself to discuss, seriously, some non-detention-based future for Kaunda.

Of course, any deal struck between the three men was not announced. Speculation had it that Kaunda would retire, if not from politics, from leadership of UNIP. As if news of this deal had been leaked, the week before saw furious jockeying for key positions with UNIP itself.

Simultaneously, Zambia had been placed under intense international pressures on other fronts. The Angolan Government complained bitterly and publicly over arms shipments to UNITA from Zambian ministerial sources; and, in a stringently-worded private note to Chiluba, named three of the most culpable. Although, in public, distancing himself from the 'private' activities of his ministers, and shrugging his shoulders at the suggestion he should be his brothers' keeper, he did, in cabinet, order an end to such shipments. Meanwhile, various diplomatic sources in Lusaka, impressed by the language used in Angola's private note, speculated on a possible 'hot pursuit' by the Angolan Government of UNITA rebels deeply enough into Zambian territory to reinforce, in the most barbed way, a basic point. However, in restraining his ministers, Chiluba has lost some of his flexibility. The internal politesse of the upper echelons of government seems very much to be that the president commands political support in return for licences to indulge in personal gain. Apart from corruption, that has included drug and gem smuggling; but gun-running for the benefit of the opponents of a neighbouring government seems now to have been brought to a temporary end. One wonders, however, whether there are, in general terms, any parameters to the relentless quest for gain.

Under the constitution that rose from the Indonesian moment of 1990, Chiluba is limited to two presidential terms. Whether he might seek a constitutional change is open to question. However, even if he has now effectively diminished or neutered his greatest opposition threats, there are many in the MMD, some more fancifully than others, who would like to be president. Kaunda was from the east of the country (or, according to the MMD official line, from east of the country entirely, i.e. Malawi); Chiluba is from the northern Bemba people. Many of the aspirants are also Bemba so, under the sense of balance introduced by Kaunda, they must satisfy the Lozi west and the Tonga south that their futures will be safeguarded - those areas, at the moment, having no obvious presidential candidates in their midsts. So, under the surface, proto-campaigns have begun. Michael Sata, a ruthless operator and consummate politician, seems an early front-runner, happily and easily choking off support to junior rivals, seeming to anticipate an eventual clash of heavyweights - possible with Godfrey Miyanda, a former vice-president, perhaps one of the only uncorrupt members of government, who has been forging with Christian groups, both to reinforce the halo of righteousness and to reach out to the poor who, as everywhere, seek solace in charismatic prayer and song. Whether either man accepts technocratic advice easily is a difficult question. Certainly, a Sata government would be even more authoritarian than anything Zambia has previously known. It would have, however, perhaps a greater sense of realism and not make so many false moves.

With the exit of Chongwe, there is no obvious technocratic leader to contest the stakes. The closest may be former Health Minister, Dr Bonface Kawimbe, a brilliant doctor and medical entrepreneur, who, in the first two years of the first MMD Government, made an imaginative national health policy work. He may be fondly remembered for his efforts, but memories can be very short when serious campaigning begins - with its promises and threats. Kawimbe has no power base, can forge no real alliances, can promise no immediate patronage, and probably does not have it in him to wage a war of threats. A long shot, but the technocrats are few in number now - the MMD has not been kind to them - and Kawimbe at least has attracted Sata's baleful attention. Whether that is a good or bad thing for Kawimbe remains to be seen.

Meanwhile, the MMD has made overtures to the remnants of the opposition for forms of dialogue. The strategy has seemed to be to crush the main players, then incorporate the small fish. In the absence of actual opposition from the opposition, non-governmental groups concerned with governance have adopted more confrontational roles, drawn into the vacuum the emasculated opposition has left. The Americans have made clear their admiration for such groups; and the Scandinavians have agreed to fund their work; but their tactics are naive, and the government seems content, at this stage, to play psychological wars of harassment and misrepresentation of their leaders.

For now, the battleground is within the MMD itself. It always would have been. Chiluba, if he had let him stand, would have defeated Kaunda at the 1996 polls. A defeated Kaunda, as opposed to a 'wronged' Kaunda, would have had less to confer upon a gentlemanly lawyer like Chongwe. Mung'omba could never have won the presidency either. Why crush those who could not win? Only by seeking to crush Kaunda in 1996 did Chiluba raise Kaunda's profile. If he had not done that, he would not have needed to seek to crush him again on Christmas Day 1997. For now, after much government effort, Chongwe and Mung'omba are probably out of the frame for the 2001 elections. Whether Kaunda remains a force in 2001 depends upon the deal Mandela negotiated for his release. In any case, Chiluba is unlikely to reverse the constitutional amendments that prevented Kaunda running for president in 1996. By 2001, it will have been ten years since the fruit of Zambia's Indonesian moment first took office. It can be said to have tried hard for up to two years. Then, power, parochiality and paranoia ate the revolution.

Reprise

In the last week of May, up to 2000 Zimbabwean students besieged parliament in a direct emulation of what Indonesian students briefly also did. They chanted 'Suharto, Mugabe, Indonesia, Zimbabwe!' in both a clear comparison and expressing clear hope. But only a year ago, the Harare township chant was 'Me, Mo, Moi, Mu!', meaning Mengistu (overthrown), Mobutu (overthrown), Moi (whom many hoped would be overthrown in Kenya, but wasn't), and Mugabe (whom the chanters now saw as a president in Moi's mould, and this was not meant to be complimentary). The wits and protesters of Harare had a sense of regionalism and internationalism; but, as one leader gives way to another elsewhere, Mugabe remains. And, unlike Moi's Kenya, no meaningful opposition - even if fragmented in Kenya, it was at least large - is organized in Zimbabwe. Change, as suggested earlier, must emanate from some wing of the present ZANU (PF).

Interestingly, Suharto had advised both Mugabe and Chiluba. Something of a father-figure to incumbents seeking presidential longevity, he had cautioned Chiluba against relying so heavily upon IMF and World Bank funds (Suharto knew what he was talking about here). The result, according to Zambian sources, was the introduction of a local fuel levy which has, finally, permitted the repair of Lusaka's downtown roads (although the Kafue road, relaid two years ago, with World Bank finance, to Swedish specifications, is showing signs of breaking up; there is not enough seasonal snow in Lusaka to keep the tarmac as compact as in Sweden). So, if the students of Zimbabwe have an Indonesian image in mind, various leaders in southern Africa probably have more interest in such metaphors than might be supposed.

There is very little real work done on how leaders from such disparate regions, meeting rarely, and often only at multilateral summits such as the Non-Aligned Movement, can establish such friendly commonalties.[10] But if democratic movements spread by example, modes of facilitation of authoritarian rule also spread by advice and example. If Suharto fell, others learn, or at least seek to learn, how to avoid the fall.

CODA

The students of Harare could not succeed in May 1998. The price rises of January 1998 had not been repeated. Unlike Indonesia, there was no vacilliation in either police force or army. Tsvangirai was not ready to play his hand. And, if an Indonesian moment had been exactly won, no wanted either of the two vice-presidents to succeed Mugabe - Joshua Nkomo is old and sick; Simon Mudenza is also old, and embroiled in a controversy involving monies he owes to a failed bank.

If it is Mugabe and, in Zambia, Chiluba for the short terms - until 2002 And 2001 respectively - and, if they do not contest, i.e. do not overcome internal party opposition to contest the elections in those years, what does the mid-term future hold? The present author believes, the hopes of reformist technocrats and intellectuals in both countries notwithstanding, there will be the advent of even harder men in both capitals. However, unlike the present incumbents, they will make more show of safeguarding procedural democracy. They will make fewer false moves while harassing, more systematically, but in lower key, opposition figures - whom they will certainly not imprison. Sophistication in this sphere will move up a notch.

Similarly, these strong, authoritarian figures, while not stamping down on corruption as a culture, will establish parameters to it - on the understanding that, taken beyond a certain, still lucrative, point, it causes longer-term difficulties for government and the trade in corruption itself. Less but sustained longer will be the new politesse here.

ZANU (PF) and the MMD will bind their feuding wings together. To feud over power is better than, because divided, to feud out of power. But, within power, powerplays being what they are and, in times of duress, perhaps future attempts at Indonesian moments racking up points even against hard men, there may be a need to make sacrificial lambs of the leaders of the immediate past - just as Chiluba has, clumsily, sought to do with Kaunda. One day, the present sins of the fathers will be hoisted on political gibbets by the hard sons. Who, on the jacaranda and flame-flower-strewn streets will chant a dirge of mourning then?

Notes and References

[1]*Herald* (Harare), 29 June 1990

[2]*Parade* (Harare), April 1992, p.39

[3]Chongwe was, *inter alia*, six years Chairperson of the Law Association of Zambia, and had also been President of the African Bar Association, and President of the Commonwealth Lawyers Association. He had been Minister of Legal Affairs, then Local Government, in the MMD Government. When he fell out with Chiluba, the Zambian Government could, at that time, have nominated him to the International Court of Justice and, thus, removed a thorn from its side, but could not bring itself to stomach the prestige this would have conferred on Chongwe.

[4]See Stephen Chan, *Kaunda and Southern Africa,* London I.B. Tauris, 1992, especially. Chapters 2 and 5; however, for more detailed study of a period of 'scientific' policy, in this case foreign policy , see Douglas Anglin, *Zambian Crisis Behaviour*, Montreal : McGill - Queens University Press, 1994.

[5] A pretty exact description of Mandaza's then publishing base - although, in a bald irony, he made this statement in one of Mandaza's own journals. Quoted in *Southern African Review of Books*, Vol. 5 No1. issue 23, 1993. p.19

[6] Terrence Ranger, *Peasant Consciousness and Guerrilla War in Zimbabwe*, London : James Currey, 1985; David Lan, *Guns & Rain : Guerrillas and Spirit Mediums in Zimbabwe*, James Currey: London : 1985; Norma Kriger, 'The Zimbabwean War of Liberation : Struggles within the Struggle', *Journal of Modern African Studies*, Vol. 14, 1988.

[7] Quoted in the *Guardian* (London), 24 January 1998.

[8] Such literature as exists has had its own genealogy, from S.E.Finer, *The Man on Horseback*, London : Pall Mall Press, 1962; to recent work on democracy and military roles within it. See Larry Diamond, Juan. Linz & Seymour Martin Lipset (eds.), *Politics in Developing Countries*, Boulder : Lynne Rienner, 1990. In between, there have been all manner of unusual approaches to build models of civil-military relations, some more well-known than others, e.g. Yaw Agyeman-Badu & Kwaku Osei-Hwedie, *The Political Economy of Instability*, Laurenceville : Brunswick, 1982; and revisionist tracts, e.g. Stephen Chan, 'The Study of African Coups - Some Notes for a Fresh Approach', *Royal United Services Institute Journal for Defence Studies*, Vol. 129 No.4, 1984. However, nothing deeply investigates the link indicated in the text, above. 'Relative deprivation' is a term coined by Ted Gurr, *Why Men Rebel*, Princeton : Princeton University Press, 1970.

[9] *Economist* (London), 3 January 1998, p.51.

[10]See, however, Paul Brooker, *Twentieth-Century Dictatorships : The Ideological One-Party States*, London :Macmillan, 1995, for an effort to establish some more than obvious commonalties between parties, if not leaders.

POSTSCRIPT:

A NOTE ON THE FUTURE AND PAST OF ZAMBIA: SEPTEMBER 1999

In September 1999, the millennium closing, there was still a nostalgia for Kaunda. The wearily-voiced opinions on the Lusaka streets were expressing just that, however: a nostalgia. Things might have seemed better, certainly less corrupt and therefore more equitable, when the Old Man was in power; but a new world has visited Zambia since then, and everyone knows it. Still, there is enough support for him at least to contemplate contesting the next elections, even though the future is elsewhere, even though his eligibility, on the grounds that he is in fact Malawian, is still contested. The counter-accusations, that Chiluba is also Malawian, have also not disappeared, and this appears a delicate card that Chiluba's government has chosen to play.

Opinion in neighbouring Zimbabwe is, as ever, airily superior on this question. By the strictest of boundary measures, Mugabe might even be Mozambican. Who cares? The boundaries of colonialism were exactly those permeated by the choice of affiliations and the track-record and risks taken for that affiliation. Even now, villages on the Mozambique side of the boarder consider themselves by orientation and population. Zimbabwean. Chimoio is as Zimbabwean a town as any in Zimbabwe itself.

The narrow political games played in Zambia are paralleled only by the extravagant carelessness of private corruptions. Angola almost went to war with Zambia in the last year over the gun-running of senior Zambian ministers to UNITA, without hindrance from Chiluba until the Angolans commenced some rather noisy sabre rattling.

It was said, on the streets of Lusaka that, had the coup attempt of the previous year succeeded, Angola would have been the first government to recognise and, indeed support the rebels. In September 1999, 95 soldiers were condemned to death for their part in the coup attempt. Chiluba declined to consider clemency at that moment, commenting that this was within the province of the judiciary – and, in fact, the appeals process could run for up to another two years. Clemency on the eve of 2001 elections would be a tidy little publicity coup of Chiluba's own. Kaunda also used to grant clemency, even though it is often forgotten how long he would take to do it, reducing his opponents within prison regimes that are still uncivilised.

The pro-democracy non-governmental action groups did not dispute the court's guilty verdict, but confined themselves to commentary on the desirability of abolishing capital punishment. They seem to have given the government an easier ride in 1999 than previously.

Internationally, Chiluba has sought to succeed Kaunda in conflict mediation. Hardly successful in Angola, he has had only a succession of illusory breakthroughs in the Democratic Republic of Congo. Something may still come of that, but only when the belligerents are ready. Here, unlike Clausewitz, diplomacy has become an extension of war, and the Congolese war is for the giant stakes of partitioning a huge and hugely rich country, ending instability on a huge number of frontiers and, in the east, perhaps settling the Hutu/Tutsi problem forever – to the perpetual disadvantage of the Hutu. To become mired in the diplomacy of this cauldron, Chiluba would have needed better advisers than he has, and greater personal adroitness. He still doesn't **seem** presidential, and the presidential ghost of Kaunda is understandably irksome. Irksomeness is hardly a foundation for policy, however, and it is a great disappointment to the early international and, indeed, national supporters of the MMD that the illusion, at least, of graciousness has disappeared from government.

Meanwhile, Chiluba's advisers and ministers keep manoeuvering for the succession. Rumours continue that Chiluba might attempt a third term, under the somewhat contentious rubric that the constitutional limitation of two presidential terms was only introduced some time after the MMD came to power and he is, therefore, entitled to two terms from that date. His supporters do not talk about the spirit of the constitution, and it is good spirit that has been disbanded in Zambian politics. The barons would not want the present King to stand again, but the barons must not quarrel among themselves so much that the King has as easy run between them all. As it is, South African President Mbeki seems to have, at 1999's end, persuaded Chiluba not to run.

Kaunda, rightly or wrongly, once projected a notion of nobility in Zambia. His supporters suspect that if, despite all, he is elected president again in 2001 – having had himself many more than two terms – he knows himself old enough and untechnocratic enough in today's world to represent an entire future. He will, they say, resign shortly into his term in favour of a younger, more technocratic person. Who this might be is as much a parlour game as which baron will be the heir to Chiluba. UNIP, Kaunda's party is not replete with talent. Rodger Chongwe, an erstwhile ally, is still in an Australian exile. Kaunda's son, Wezi, was assassinated towards the end of 1999, thus ending that heir apparent. It will almost certainly be the MMD again, but who leads the MMD will form the only substantial question in the next two years.

And what can that person do? Zambia, despite IMF and World Bank notices, is simply not the Ghana of Jerry Rawlings. There just isn't the continuity of a judicious economic liberalism, with the discipline of expenditures within government. Privatisation, far from providing alternative avenues for corruption, as it were, has merely fuelled a feeding-frenzy among ministers to be corrupt in government, to finance their private sector speculations. The use of ministries has become a free market in itself. To that extent, Zambia is in line to become a Kenya. There is one saving grace: there will not be a huge ring of shanties around Lusaka. The majority of Zambia is urbanised already. Kaunda's 'welfare state' initiatives provided the nuclei of orderly, even if now under - provisioned, public services in the poorer suburbs. So the extremes of Kenyan wealth will be more modestly extreme in Zambia; but they will be extreme enough. It is hard to live, as an ordinary citizen. Once fallen from the lower middle class, and life becomes the most sophisticated ingenuity imaginable. It is, however, the lower middle class the ministers rob and despoil and not those organized and educated enough to petition for assistance.

That's the nucleus of rebellion in the army. Certainly not strong enough to stand before a battle-hardened Angolan onslaught, it is an army with a memory of a lower middle class origin or aspiration. It is the relatives and families of the rank and file who are at risk. One day, an organized coup may, undrunkenly, situate itself before a president's office. It is the only Anglophonic State in southern Africa where this could happen. It would not be junior soldiers facing the hangman then.

To be cynical (or hopeful), the penchant for opportunistic distraction – alcohol and sex – may be both a bane and salvation of a recognisable polity and government. As with soldiers staging a coup, or athletes on the eve of a continental games; as with ministers looting a budget; as with privatised businesses without contingency recognitions – the terrifying aspect of Zambia is that ridiculous balance of wayward forces, by which each recognises the other, exploited and exploiter alike, and which, by his self-presentation at least, if not genuine impulse, the Old Ghost of Zambia, Kaunda, once seemed to transcend. He was, in many ways a ridiculous man. In some ways, he was the best man who ever walked that dusty stage. I have both praised and criticised him in these pages, and in others published elsewhere. I must say now: it is not his rivals who will have such books written about them.

INDEX

AFRICAN STUDIES

1. Karla Poewe, **The Namibian Herero: A History of Their Psychosocial Disintegration and Survival**
2. Sara Joan Talis (ed. and trans.), **Oral Histories of Three Secondary School Students in Tanzania**
3. Randolph Stakeman, **The Cultural Politics of Religious Change: A Study of the Sanoyea Kpelle in Liberia**
4. Ayyoub-Awaga Bushara Gafour, **My Father the Spirit-Priest: Religion and Social Organization in the Amaa Tribe (Southwestern Sudan)**
5. Rosalind I. J. Hackett (ed.), **New Religious Movements in Nigeria**
6. Irving Hexham, **Texts on Zulu Religion: Traditional Zulu Ideas About God**
7. Alexandre Kimenyi, **Kinyarwanda and Kirundi Names: A Semiolinguistic Analysis of Bantu Onomastics**
8. G. C. Oosthuizen, (*et al*), **Afro-Christian Religion and Healing in Southern Africa**
9. Karla Poewe, **Religion, Kinship, and Economy in Luapula, Zambia**
10. Mario Azevedo (ed.), **Cameroon and Chad in Historical and Contemporary Perspectives**
11. John E. Eberegbulam Njoku, **Traditionalism Versus Modernism at Death: Allegorical Tales of Africa**
12. David Hirschmann, **Changing Attitudes of Black South Africans Toward the United States**
13. Panos Bardis, **South Africa and the Marxist Movement: A Study in Double Standards**
14. John E. Eberegbulam Njoku, **The Igbos of Nigeria: Ancient Rites, Changes and Survival**
15. Aliyu Alhaji Idrees, **Domination and Reaction in Nupeland, Central Nigeria: The Kyadya Revolt, 1857-1905**
16. Kenoye Kelvin Eke, **Nigeria's Foreign Policy Under Two Military Governments, 1966-1979: An Analysis of the Gowan and Muhammed/Obasanjo Regimes**
17. Herbert Ekwe-Ekwe, **The Biafra War: Nigeria and the Aftermath**

18. I. D. Talbott, **Agricultural Innovation in Colonial Africa: Kenya and the Great Depression**
19. G. C. Oosthuizen and Irving Hexham (eds.), **Afro-Christian Religion at the Grassroots in Southern Africa**
20. Bessie House-Midamba, **Class Development and Gender Inequality in Kenya, 1963-1990**
21. David Owusu-Ansah, **Islamic Talismanic Tradition in Nineteenth-Century Asante**
22. Segun Gbadegesin (ed.), **The Politicization of Society During Nigeria's Second Republic, 1979-1983**
23. Tukumbi Lumumba-Kasongo, **Nationalistic Ideologies, Their Policy Implications and the Struggle for Democracy in African Politics**
24. Getachew Metaferia and Maigenet Shifferraw, **The Ethiopian Revolution of 1974 and the Exodus of Ethiopia's Trained Human Resources**
25. George Cotter, **Proverbs and Sayings of the Oromo People of Ethiopia and Kenya with English Translations**
26. J. W. T. Allen, Roland Allen, N. Q. King, Jan Knappert, et al. (eds.), **A Poem Concerning the Death of the Prophet Muhammad /** ***Utendi Wa Kutawafu Nabii***
27. Salah M. Hassan, **Art and Islamic Literacy Among the Hausa of Northern Nigeria**
28. Samuel S. Simbandwe, **A Socio-Religious and Political Analysis of the Judeo-Christian Concept of Prophetism and Modern Bakongo and Zulu African Prophet Movements**
29. Pyare L. Arya, **Structure, Policies and Growth Prospects of Nigeria**
30. Sheikh Batu Daramy, **Constitutional Developments in the Post-Colonial State of Sierra-Leone 1961-1984**
31. Abiodun Goke-Pariola, **The Role of Language in the Struggle for Power and Legitimacy in Africa**
32. Marjorie H. Stewart, **Borgu and its Kingdoms: A Reconstruction of Western Sudanese Polity**
33. Abdalla Uba Adamu, **Reform and Adaptation in Nigerian University Curricula 1960-1992: Living on the Credit Line**
34. Thomas M. Shaw, **The Fulani Matrix of Beauty and Art in the Djolof Region of Senegal**

35. Toyin Falola, A. Ajayi, A. Alao, B. Babawale, **The Military Factor in Nigeria 1966-1985**
36. Samba Diop, **The Oral History and Literature of the Wolof People of Waalo, Northern Senegal: The Master of the Word (Griot) in the Wolof Tradition**
37. Rina Okonkwo, **Protest Movements in Lagos, 1908-1930**
38. Felton Best (editor), **Black Resistance Movements in the United States and Africa, 1800-1993**
39. Jeffrey C. Stone, **A Short History of the Cartography of Africa**
40. H.L. Pretorius, **Historiography and Historical Sources Regarding African Indigenous Churches in South Africa**
41. Michael Okema, **Political Culture of Tanzania**
42. Alven Makapela, **The Problem with Africanity in the Seventh-Day Adventist Church**
43. Patrick E. Idoye, **Theatre and Social Change in Zambia: The Chikwakwa Theatre**
44. M.C. Kitshoff (ed.), **African Independent Churches Today: Kaleidoscope of Afro-Christianity**
45. Charles O. Chikeka, **Decolonization Process in Africa During the Post-War Era, 1960-1990**
46. Santosh C. Saha, **Culture in Liberia: An Afrocentric View of the Cultural Interaction Between the Indigenous Liberians and the Americo-Liberians**
47. John Mukum Mbaku (ed.), **Corruption and the Crisis of Institutional Reforms in Africa**
48. Immaculate N. Kizza, **Africa's Indigenous Institutions in Nation Building: Uganda**
49. Tayo Oke, **Radicalism, Political Power and Foreign Policy in Nigeria**
50. Wayne Madsen, **Genocide and Covert Operations in Africa, 1993-1999**
51. Jim Ocitti, **Political Evolution and Democratic Practice in Uganda 1952-1996**
52. Gary Y. Okihiro, **A Social History of the Bakwena and Peoples of the Kalahari of Southern Africa, 19th Century**
53. Ritchard Tamba M'Bayo, Chuka Onwumechili, R. Nwafo Nwanko (eds.), **Press and Politics in Africa**

54. Thomas K. Ranuga, **South Africa Under Majority Rule: A Study in Power Sharing, Racial Equality and Democracy**
55. Graham Harrison, **The Politics of Democratisation in Rural Mozambique: Grassroots Governance in Mecúfi**
56. Amir H. Idris, **Sudan's Civil War–Slavery, Race and Formational Identities**
57. Stephen Chan, **Zambia and the Decline of Kaunda 1984-1998,** Craig Clancy (ed.)